WHO WRITES THIS CRAP?

Joel Stickley is a writer and performer. His work has been featured on Radio 4, Radio 3, BBC7, BBC Scotland and BBC Choice, which doesn't exist any more but did at the time. As a member of Aisle16, he has performed at Glastonbury, the Edinburgh Fringe, Port Eliot Lit Fest, the Latitude festival and a whole clutch of literary events across the country. Aisle16's comedy theatre show *Poetry Boyband* was named as *Time Out*'s Critics' Choice of the Year in 2005.

Luke Wright is best known as a poet. He is a 2007 *4Talent* Award Winner, the founder of Aisle16 and the host and programmer of Latitude's poetry programme, which is the biggest gathering of live poets in the UK. He has been described by the *Observer* as 'the best young performance poet around'. For more information visit lukewright.co.uk.

WHO WRITES THIS CRAP?

ALL THE RUBBISH YOU READ IN A DAY – REWRITTEN

Joel Stickley & Luke Wright

PENGUIN BOOKS

Published by the Penguin Group

Penguin Books Ltd, 80 Strand, London WC2R 0RL, England

Penguin Group (USA) Inc., 375 Hudson Street, New York, New York 10014, USA

Penguin Group (Canada), 90 Eglinton Avenue East, Suite 700, Toronto,
Ontario, Canada M4P 2Y3
(a division of Pearson Penguin Canada Inc.)

Penguin Ireland, 25 St Stephen's Green, Dublin 2, Ireland (a division of Penguin Books Ltd)

Penguin Group (Australia), 250 Camberwell Road,
Camberwell, Victoria 3124, Australia (a division of Pearson Australia Group Pty Ltd)

Penguin Books India Pvt Ltd, 11 Community Centre,
Panchsheel Park, New Delhi – 110 017, India

Penguin Group (NZ), 67 Apollo Drive, North Shore 0632,
New Zealand (a division of Pearson New Zealand Ltd)

Penguin Books (South Africa) (Pty) Ltd, 24 Sturdee Avenue,
Rosebank, Johannesburg 2196, South Africa

Penguin Books Ltd, Registered Offices: 80 Strand, London WC2R 0RL, England

www.penguin.com

First published by Hamish Hamilton 2007
Published in Penguin Books 2008
1

Copyright © Joel Stickley and Luke Wright, 2007
All rights reserved

978–0–141–03054–8

www.greenpenguin.co.uk

Penguin Books is committed to a sustainable future
for our business, our readers and our planet.
The book in your hands is made from paper
certified by the Forest Stewardship Council.

For Fran, to whom I owe a great deal. Of course, if that
was the only criterion, I'd be dedicating it to the Halifax.

– JS

To Sally, for the endless hours spent listening to my crap.

– LW

OPTIMO HAIRFLOW TEA TREE, JOJOBA AND HAKE SHAMPOO

is infused with a subtle blend of fragrances designed to invigorate, enliven and inspire. After just three weeks using it twice a day, you'll be feeling so much extra confidence that your life will improve immeasurably in every way. You will find discarded money in gutters. You will win competitions you didn't even enter. You will almost certainly get a promotion at work. Using OPTIMO HAIRFLOW SHAMPOO will actually be earning you money, which makes that extra 60p a bottle over the supermarket's own-brand shampoo seem more than worthwhile. In fact, it might be wise to invest your newfound wealth in buying more OPTIMO HAIRFLOW SHAMPOO. This will give you a further boost of self-worth, spurring you on to even greater heights and allowing you to purchase yet more OPTIMO products. Ultimately, this process will result in you having dominion over all the peoples of the earth and issuing commands from the highest minaret of your solid gold palace, where you bathe all day in a vast Olympic-sized swimming pool of shampoo, looking down on the lowly masses beneath you and laughing and laughing and laughing.

For best results, use with
OPTIMO HAIRFLOW CONDITIONER.
Avoid contact with eyes,
teeth and lawyers.

SCUFF®
Foaming Shave Gel
for the closest wet shave

Directions for use: Apply Foaming Shave Gel to your rugged face. Shave. Then seize the day. Grab it roughly by the shirt collar and say, "I know you and I like your work, but as of today you answer directly to this face." As you say this, point to your own face – the one you've just shaved using Scuff Foaming Shave Gel. Let the day briefly touch your face and admire its smoothness. Rinse and repeat.

WARNING: For male use only – Scuff Foaming Shave Gel can melt a lady's skin.

Full Fair
Deep Roast Coffee

~

Our Promise

We source all the ingredients for Full Fair Deep Roast Coffee in an ethical and sustainable way, ensuring the best possible deal for the farmers and factory workers who produce it. In fact, the arrangement we have with the farmers and workers is so unusually preferential that we feel slightly aggrieved at paying so much for a product which we could be getting elsewhere for a fraction of the cost. Luckily, we can pass this deficit on to you, the consumer, by adding the words "Fair" and "Promise" to the packaging and increasing the price. You get to feel good about yourself, the farmers can afford to emigrate somewhere with better labour laws and, most importantly, our profit margins remain intact. With this in mind, we solemnly promise that we will always continue to offer ethically traded alternatives alongside our standard products until such time as this whole fad blows over and it becomes unprofitable for us to do so.

Malt Flakes

Take the *Malt Flakes* Challenge with Malt Flakes – the nation's favourite flakes of malt – and lose 90% of your body fat in just three weeks. All you need is one bowl of malt flakes for breakfast,* three double espressos for lunch and two Turbo-Lax tablets for dinner.

Nutritional expert Jane Horton-Starkie explains: "The *Malt Flakes* Challenge is like no diet I've ever seen. Its effects are drastic, immediate and quite possibly irreversible."

Unlike most diets, the *Malt Flakes* Challenge does not place restrictions on all food types. Water, for example, is NOT off-limits.

* Do not add milk.

Nutritional Information

One 378g serving of Malt Flakes will provide you with 400% of your recommended daily intake of get-up-and-go-itude.

120% RDA refined sugar, 90% RDA saturated fats, 7% RDA tallow.

Serving Suggestion

To improve your health and our legal position, why not try eating Malt Flakes as part of a balanced diet?

Malt Flakes are produced in the UK under licence by:
Axis Chemicals International, 16 Reclamation Road, Luton

Hiya!

Drinking another SupaDupaWupa Smoothie? Good on you! Aren't they just brill? (Wait, don't answer that, we already know!) SupaDupaWupa Smoothies are made from 100% fruit and marketing hype. Nothing else. Go on – test us. Come round to Pear Top House and test us. We'll be here waiting for you, playing table tennis and talking about fruit, so why not drop round? Doubt is something we're used to, haters we can handle, but before you question us, just take a moment to think: how will this affect the fruit? That's all we ask, because fruit is innocent and pure, and hate is the opposite. Sure, it might seem like a great idea for you to come round here and start 'testing' us, but where will that lead? A brief look into the future and what do we see? SupaDupaWupa Smoothies – made from 100% fruit and marketing hype . . . oh, and a huge great dollop of hate. Nice one, doubter.

Keep on Juicing!

The Fruit Gang

Competition

Hey there! We're just totally fruity about fruit down here at Pear Top House. That's why we're launching a fruit-tastic competition. We want you to send us pictures of your favourite fruit. Use crayons, felt tips, even a bit of glitter if you like. The best ones will be printed on our cartons and you'll win a free smoothie. Yay!

Send your entries to: SupaDupaWupa, Pear Top House,
The Fruit Loop, The Little Apple, PO Box 123756738, London.

Ingredients

Fruit, a David & Goliath back story, a good relationship with the creative media, saccharin.

Clear® – You're In Ambitious Hands™

October 07

Your Last Bill
Amount charged   £68.95
Amount paid   £68.95 (cheers – we owe you one!)

Your Latest Bill
Outstanding balance   £0.00 (nice one, see above)
Your monthly plan charges   £42.17 (pretty reasonable, considering)
Charges outside plan   £30.34 (someone likes ringtones!)
Total Balance   £72.51

Progressive **VAT***
Charged at 23.5% on £72.51   £17.04

Amount Due   £89.55

We will come round and collect this money on or around 25/11/07

* Progressive VAT is charged at 23.5% and not the archaic 17.5% that some companies still insist on
patronising their customers with. VAT stands for Value Added Tax. Clear® offer a whopping 6% more
value than the industry norm of 17.5%. It's good to know you're in ambitious hands.

Personal Report for Customer W-00-978651

Texting
No real problems here. Customer W-00-978651 seems to have grasped the basic concept. He's applied himself well to learning the fundamentals of text language, although a few time-saving idiosyncrasies still escape him. On 14/09/07, despite a number of Clear® Text Alerts on the subject of "More Speed, Less Haste", he sent a garbled, vowel-less message to 07281735872 which resulted in a phone call of 9m34s – hardly a time-saving technique! Normally, we at Clear® wouldn't mind, but the caller was on another service provider, so in this instance Customer W-00-978651 caused one of our competitors to profit. Not really the sort of behaviour we want to see again in the future. Still, there is much to be pleased with; he's excelled at text flirting and this could yet lead to a date or two. Keep up the good work!

Bill Paying
Pleasing progress. Direct Debit seems to be working.

Phone Calls
Customer W-00-978651 is a perfectly able conversationalist. This was evident on 10/09/07 when he spoke to 07134457234 for 56m31s and on 23/09/07 when he put in an impressive 1h45m02s to 07143567294. Put simply: we know he can do it. It's just that most of the time he doesn't seem to try. This is the second month running that he hasn't exceeded his call limit and quite frankly we're worried. It's all very well playfully flirting with a well-worded text but soon she'll want to talk about "feelings" and "joint accounts". If he continues to present these monosyllabic answers (cf. 26/09/07 0m34s to 07236462845), he might find himself with one less speed-dial. The time to act is now. Come on, Customer W-00-978651, pull your finger out.

Downloads
Excels at games and ringtones, but his insistence on replying to automated text alerts is costing him money and us time.

WAP, Premium Numbers and Other Services
We've encountered customers like Customer W-00-978651 before: perfectly content to keep hitting redial but too nervous to try something new. A phone is not just about keeping in touch with friends and loved ones; it's a slickly designed, palm-sized key into a world of online gambling, sex chat lines and a plethora of Indian call centres. Take ANSATXT for example – an independent company owned, controlled and regulated by Clear®. All you have to do is text them your question* on 80123 and the experts at ANSATXT will get back to you within 72 working hours with their answer.** This month, we'd really like to see Customer W-00-978651 getting stuck into more premium-rate services like ANSATXT. Remember, "premium" can mean good as well as expensive.

* Questions cost £2.00
** Answers cost between £0.50 & £4.50

Clear® – You're In Ambitious Hands™

FAQ

Q Why are there charges on my bill that I don't recognise?

A Occasionally you might not recognise a charge for a service or download even though you definitely ordered it. This is because the process of mobile telecommunications billing is a multifaceted and intricate process that mere customers can never hope to fully understand. But consider this: do you fully understand the equation $E=MC^2$? No, of course not. Why should you? But you agree with everyone when they say Einstein was a clever guy, right? Of course you do. I wouldn't worry about it if I were you.

Q Can I get a copy of this bill with a pink letterhead instead of a grey one?

A You sure can! Just log on to www. clearmeout.com/letterheads and set your bill preferences.

Q I rang you up and got stuck listening to "Greensleeves" on repeat for seven hours! Something's got to give! Can't you change it to the Pussycat Dolls or something?

A We already have done. Now when you call Clear® you have a choice of "Greensleeves" or the Pussycat Dolls (and don't forget to check out our exclusive range of Pussycat Dolls merchandise on www.clearmeout.com).

Q Can I get a copy of this bill in Braille?

A Probably. But for an extra £6.99, you can have your bill read to you by the voice of Carol Vorderman.

Q I love you, Clear®. How can I show my appreciation?

A That's so sweet of you. As it happens, we have an Amazon wishlist at www.amazon.co.uk.

Contact Us

Website: www.clearmeout.com

Address: Customer Services, Clear (UK) Ltd, 51, Shiv Market, Masjid Road, Calcutta.

E-mail: Win the chance to e-mail us direct by entering the free prize draw at www.clearmeout.com/mail

Phone: Call 100 from your mobile and hold.

Office of Communications

OFCOM is the regulator of the UK telecommunications industry and a bunch of uptight control freaks. If you really have to write to them, you can get them at: OFCOM, Blah Blah Blah Blah Blah, London, Blah Blah 19 Blah Blah.

Easy Ways to Pay

Direct Debit – With direct debit, your bill is paid each month directly from your bank account and no one has to worry about things like hassle, stress and extortionate (yet legal) late-payment fees. Just call us on 100 and we'll set it up for you. If you're using one of the payment methods below, there's a £3.00 charge to cover "payment processing" and we're likely to suspend parts of your service on a whim. So why not sign up for direct debit today?

Telephone or Internet Banking – Just enter Clear® as a regular payee to your bank account. Remember, this can take up to seven or eight working weeks to clear, so is it really worth it?

Credit or Debit Card – Call us on 100 from your Clear® phone or pop into one of our Retail Experience Areas to pay us the old-fashioned, no-nonsense way with chip and pin.

We accept *MasterCard*, *Visa*, *Amex*, *Switch*, *Delta*, *Solo*, or bribes.

Keen to be Green

Dear Resident,

As the twenty-first century begins, we all have a responsibility to look after the planet that has looked after us for so many generations. It's a bit like when your parents get old and can't look after themselves and you have to put them in a home. This can be a difficult, costly and traumatic experience for all concerned, leading to feelings of guilt and bitter recriminations with siblings who, despite being far better-off than yourself, refuse to contribute their fair share of the cost.

With this in mind, the **Keen to be Green** initiative has recently been extended into your area. In the next few weeks, each resident will receive seven plastic boxes in varying shades of green. These are your **Planet Saver Boxes**, each of which is specially designed for a different type of household waste. It's simple: just load up each box with the appropriate items, leave them out on the driveway next to your 4x4 and sit back, safe in the knowledge that you've just fulfilled your responsibility to humanity and no one can ask you to do anything else ever again.

What Goes in Each Box

Box 1: Glass bottles, jars, broken plates.

Box 2: Cardboard, junk mail, magazines, tabloid newspapers.

Box 3: Rigid plastic, electrical goods, broadsheet newspapers.

Box 4: Compostable materials: fruit and vegetables, used teabags, pet waste, brown paper, novels (science fiction, historical romance, literary).

Box 5: Non-compostable materials: forks, hairbrushes, cycling-proficiency certificates, novels (true crime, chick-lit, horror).

Box 6: Miscellaneous: wallpaper, Kevlar body-armour, three-leaved clovers, lost cats, your aunt's glasses that she left in your bathroom, old copies of the telephone directory, cheese, ham, pineapple, photographs, prescriptions, ice, wrappers from chocolate bars, discarded pornography, aerosol canisters, holiday brochures, doorknobs, corpses.

Box 7: String.

We hope that you'll enjoy the feeling of satisfaction that comes with recycling. Failing that, we hope you feel guilty when you realise in three weeks' time that these boxes are still stacked up in the back of your shed. Most of all, though, we hope you bear in mind when the time for local elections rolls around, that we tried, we really tried, and ultimately it was you who let the side down.

Thanks for being a part of **Keen to be Green**. It's an initiative that will help to safeguard the lives of our children and our children's children in the years to come. Unless we're all underwater by Christmas, in which case please feel free to use these boxes in the construction of your raft.

Thanks so much for pitching in and doing your bit! It really means a lot to me, personally and ethically.

Love,
Paula Graham (Councillor)

ZONE C

Parking without a permit is permitted during the hours 8 a.m. to 8.15 a.m. Permit required at ALL other times. Apart from 12.15 p.m. to 12.34 p.m., when it might be all right.

ZONE C

Any car parked in Zone C without a VALID parking permit at any time should display a VALID parking permit. Parking permits can be VALIDATED by placing them on the inside of your car's front windscreen. VALID permits are only required for cars without an otherwise VALID permit. Permits required at ALL times, despite what it might say on other signs.

ZONE C

Some spaces in ZONE C do NOT require
a VALID parking permit. This does not
include the spaces immediately adjacent
to this sign.

ZONE C

INVALID parking permits decrease the chances of your car receiving a parking fine. VALID permits can reduce this risk by a further 60%.

ZONE C

I wouldn't if I were you, it's not worth the risk.

ZONE C

Look, just fuck off, will you?

POLICE

HENSGATE CONSTABULARY:
POLICE FIRST, QUESTION LATER

PHONE: 999

ENTER OUR FREE PRIZE DRAW
TO WIN AN MP3 PLAYER

WARNING!

Any baggage left unattended will be removed and destroyed, no matter how unlikely it is that fanatical terrorists waging a holy war against Western civilisation would conceal an explosive device in a bright pink Miffy rucksack.

Let's Explore the Snellingford Line!

On weekends and Bank Holidays, the busy Hensgate-to-London commuter route transforms into the peaceful and picturesque Snellingford Line, providing the perfect family sight-seeing tour.

Be wowed by the tranquil splendour of the imposing Hensgate Gas Works; marvel at the science of the Snellingford Sewage Plant – the fourth largest sewage plant in the UK; enjoy the sedate pace of life as the 33-minute commuter trains kick back to a leisurely 2hrs 14mins on your journey to the cosmopolitan "eateries" of London Paddington – the world's only station named after a much-loved children's book character.

And as if that wasn't enough, on all weekends in November and December, we're adding a "site-seeing"* bus tour to the route,** allowing families to take in the perfect still majesty of the M25 and the heavy railway maintenance work in the distance. We will then complete the journey to Paddington in an impressive 3hrs 21mins.

Enquire at the ticket office about our special Family Rover Ticket.

PRIVIRAIL

THE RAILWAY CONTRACT BIDDING EXPERTS

* Building sites, mainly.
** Compulsory.

the SENTINEL

Hayes found guilty of Samantha murder

Thirty-eight-year-old Toby Hayes was convicted today of murdering eight-year-old Samantha Keeble, whose body was found last week. Hayes, who has previous convictions, was jailed for life with a recommendation by Mr Justice Mann that he should never be released.

The judge said, "My words are going to be printed in the newspapers tomorrow, so I'm going to hyperbolise." Staring at Hayes, a freelance plumber and murderer, the judge added, "I'm going to characterise you as so utterly abominable that people will be horrified and yet at the same time very glad we have a justice system robust enough to give someone like you the punishment he deserves."

There were cheers at the Old Bailey shortly after 2.45 p.m. today, the 756th day of the trial, as the foreman delivered two guilty verdicts – one for the murder and the other for effect.

Samantha's parents embraced one another as the verdict was read out. As Hayes was led out of the court, a family friend shouted at him, "I hope your own child is brutally murdered and left to rot." The court clapped and cheered in appreciation.

On the steps outside the Old Bailey, Samantha's mother stood beside her husband and renewed her calls for "Samantha's Law", which would allow parents to shoot and kill on sight anyone they saw looking at their child in a suspicious or even encouraging way.

A Home Office minister said, "Obviously the nation's thoughts are with Little Samantha, so until this all dies down, we will make every effort to look as though we are supporting whatever it is her parents want."

The jury had deliberated for thirty seconds and reached its verdict unanimously, simultaneously and ferociously.

[continued on page 2]

OUR POLICY

We will not tolerate aggressive behaviour towards our staff. Anyone who threatens a member of the train crew physically, verbally, or by way of looking at them funny, will be prosecuted to the full extent of the law and have their ticket invalidated. They will then be charged the price of a full-fare single ticket to the next station stop. In the case of actual or grievous bodily harm, Railcard discounts will not be available.

Monkey dressed as Darwin causes airport chaos

There was widespread fear and confusion in New York's JFK International Airport late last night as what security sources described as a "highly provocative simian" was discovered in the stairwell of an air traffic control tower. All flights in and out of Terminal 3 were suspended, with many commercial airliners put into holding patterns for as long as two hours. Air traffic control staff were not informed of the exact nature of the incident until the situation had been stabilised, for fear that they would react with panic and endanger the lives of thousands of passengers. At a press conference early this morning, Security Liaison Officer Andrew Peltoff described the night's events as "terrifying", "shocking" and "over".

Early reports indicate that the monkey was discovered at 23:00 local time (04:00 GMT) by a member of the airport's cleaning staff. In a statement issued by the Federal Aviation Authority, the interloper was described as "a mammalian anthropoid simian of the order Cattarhini, clad in an imitation white beard with high-collar shirt and wide-lapelled cloth jacket." Initial fears that the monkey might have been dressed as the novelist Charles Dickens proved misguided when an expert in historical costume (working as a baggage handler) identified the outfit as that of Charles Robert Darwin, a nineteenth-century naturalist and writer.

As soon as news of the incident broke, religious and scientific groups were quick to apportion blame. With no group coming forward to claim responsibility, the hours following the incident saw accusations flying thick and fast. Influential Christian lobby group Family Under Christ's Kingdom were first to comment on events, calling the Darwin monkey "a shameless, disgusting stunt by atheist scientists trying to push the evolution agenda and corrupt our children." The scientific community was quick to respond, calling the incident "a blatant attempt by hard-line creationists to discredit and ridicule evolutionary theory." A spokesperson for the animal rights organisation Humane Humanity said the monkey was "expressing itself in the only way it knew how – through costume-based satire of mankind's follies."

All sides in this heated debate responded to criticism by increasing the volume of their initial assertions until the press conference became loud and unpleasant, and all the journalists decided to sneak out. The man from Reuters said he knew a place just round the corner that had German beer on tap and made good toasted sandwiches. For the rest of the afternoon, no one even suggested going back to the press conference.

The widespread security alert at JFK International caused many flights to be delayed, leaving some passengers stranded in the departure lounges. Those without access to reasonably priced coffee and paninis quickly descended to a state of feral savagery, scavenging the seating areas for food and forming loose-knit tribal groups based on seat allocations.

This came to an abrupt end, however, when the situation was neutralised at 23:08 local time (04:08 GMT) by Air Marshal Jack Louie, who shot the monkey nine times in the face, twice in the chest and once in the groin. He then threw the corpse into the jet intake of a Boeing 737 which was idling on a nearby runway. Eyewitnesses described the resultant gore-cloud as "a beautiful pinkish mist, like sunrise over an autumn lake."

In an emotional speech after the event, Louie spoke of the "solemn, profound, God-given duty to preserve and safeguard the liberty not only of American citizens but of all people, by locating and destroying, as thoroughly as possible, all instruments of terrorism and the causes of terror." He then told a long, rambling story about how his little sister had been scared of spiders until he had burnt down their family home in an attempt to destroy cobwebs, but by that point, no one was listening.

Art

Fuck All This, Fuck You, Fuck It And Fuck
Neil Baggerton

From the signs on the way in declaring "THIS IS NOT AN ART EXHIBIT" to the climactic final piece, "I Am Making You Think About The Nature Of Art, You Shower Of Stupid, Lazy Twats", Fuck All This, Fuck You, Fuck It And Fuck is a brave and challenging work from one of Britain's most mentioned young artists. Throughout, Baggerton uses a combination of found materials, bodily fluids and outright abuse to create a sense of post-historical ennui reminiscent of the early Tangentialists.

He pulls no punches with his most overtly political piece, "Stop Fucking Looking At Me", in which a mannequin dressed as Osama Bin Laden is arranged in a position of coitus with former US Secretary of State Madeleine Albright, who is obliged to remain as part of the exhibit after Baggerton reportedly tricked her into signing a contract by pretending it was a petition against terrorism. Elsewhere in the collection, he treads on more personal territory with the provocatively titled "thwp-pthuh-fup-fup-fup-bthwaaaaaaaa", a lifesize model of his own trachea nailed to a crucifix made of polished coal and lit from below by a series of dim three-watt bulbs. Intended to highlight the suffering of disabled sex-workers, this piece also makes reference to Baggerton's own conviction for rape, a crime for which he received three hours' community service after pleading irony.

Despite their apparent negativity, hostility and, more often than not, outright meaninglessness, there is a uniting aesthetic and clear message at the heart of all these pieces. With each manifestation of human ugliness and fear, Baggerton is communicating, albeit subliminally, his unwavering and heartfelt belief that, whatever the circumstances, no matter how difficult it might be, he should be given huge amounts of money and press attention for his work. DT

Roche Out For 5 Weeks

Arsenal ace Ferdinand Roche could be out for up to five weeks following a hamstring injury sustained during Arsenal's two-nil defeat at the hands of Charlton this weekend. That means the striker will miss next weekend's crucial top of the table battle at Old Trafford. "It is very disappointing to miss the big game at Manchester United next weekend," Roche said outside his £3 million North London home today.

As a result of the injury, he will also miss the following weekend's all-important match at home · to Liverpool. "It is very disappointing to miss the big game against Liverpool the weekend after next," he added. As if that wasn't enough, Roche will also be out of action for the following weekend's fixture, a much-anticipated clash with arch-rivals Chelsea. "It is very disappointing to miss the big game against Chelsea the weekend after the weekend after next," Roche said.

Worries were also raised over the likelihood that he will miss the match away to Reading the following weekend. "It is very disappointing to miss the big game against Reading the weekend after the weekend after the weekend after next," Roche revealed. It is also thought Arsenal are not best pleased with the prospect of being without their star for a midweek match that follows only 3 days after the Reading clash – though it is not yet known who that is against or whether it is at home or away. "I'm f**ked off about the midweek thing too," Roche added.

08:26

Entered for the Man Booker Prize

Fighting Fish In The Late-Night Laundromat

The bestselling "literary" novel by
Zoe Friel

"Not only is this book very important, it is also very
good . . . Friel is at the top of her game – witty, poignant
and looking hot in the author photograph."
The Sentinel

"Reminiscent of something you've probably never
read and something else that you've also probably
never read. I've read them, and more besides."
The Review of Books

"I'm G. P. Taylor."
G. P. Taylor

Out Now in Paperback
Penguin 2007

Xi VidiScreens™

LONDON COMES TO COMPLETE STANDSTILL AS TELEVISION SCREENS PUMP OUT EVER MORE SENSATIONALIST NEWS

*Providing news 24 hours a day
in increasingly unnecessary places*

Il Lione®

Have you ever woken up at 6 a.m., run ten miles, dived into freezing cold water, swum another six miles, dived back out again, gone twelve rounds with a heavy-weight boxing champion, won, run another ten miles, scored a match-winning goal, run another ten miles, shot something with a bow and arrow, beaten a sixteen-stone man to death with your bare hands, run another ten miles and then gone to work and not felt the need to boast?

We made this vest for you.

Il Lione®
It means lion . . . in Italian™

There was once a wise man who lived on a hill above a small village. One day, the villagers went to ask the wise man's advice, but he was not in his wooden hut. They searched for him for about ten minutes and then stopped. "What's the point?" they said. "He's gone." But one little boy refused to give up. He searched all night and all of the next day as well. Eventually, after three days of searching, he found the wise man under a box of old newspapers in his garage. He'd been dead for about a week.

Chinese Proverb

*If you could talk to anyone, anywhere, any time,
just imagine the stories they'd tell . . .*

Clear®
You're In Ambitious Hands™

NOTICE

Please do not:

- Smoke onboard the train
- Put your feet up on the seats
- Spit chewing gum on the floor
- Deface this sHIT

If you see anyone abusing the train facilities, please contact the British Transport Police by standing up and shouting, "British Transport Police! This young man has his trainers on the upholstery!" At this point, you may want to attempt a citizen's arrest. Go for an arm-lock or half-nelson. You will be a hero to your fellow passengers.

FREE PLATFORM

London's ONLY free daily newspaper with the word platform in its title

ANGEL KILLED BY SATAN

Lesley speaks out – Lesley Simms interview
page 10

Vile child-killer Toby Hayes was today convicted of killing little angel Samantha Keeble. After the foreman had read the jury's verdict, the judge calmly and heroically said to the dishevelled and sly-looking Hayes, "My words are going to be printed in the newspapers tomorrow, so I'm going to hyperbolise."

Hayes was sentenced to life in prison and the judge recommended that he never be released. Some pressure groups are now pushing for the death sentence to be reintroduced.

PLATFORM has carried out its own research, getting opinions from a random cross-section of society.

"I think we should bring back the death sentence," said Mrs C., the mother of a murdered child from Birkenhead.

"I want that man dead. And others like him." That was the stern verdict of Mr L., the husband of a woman murdered by a street gang in Essex.

"I think we should bring back capital punishment to help with the grieving process," agreed Ms P. of Surrey, the daughter of an old lady murdered by thugs.

It's bound to be controversial, but this survey does seem to suggest that people want tougher sentences for murderers.

Continued on page 4 after some cute animal stories.

ROCHE HAMSTRING INJURY – SPORT ON THE BACK

PEOPLE WHO SMILE MORE TEND TO BE HAPPIER, STUDY SUGGESTS

In a ground-breaking new study, the results of which were released today, scientists from the Institute of Behavioural Research have found a correlation between instances of smiling and the overall happiness of experimental participants. Mukash Couri, the head of IBR's research department, told assembled journalists that it was "impossible at this stage to draw definitive conclusions" but that the data showed an "unmistakable correlative trend."

The study, which was funded in part by the newly formed National Smiling Society, was intended to draw attention to issues of psychological well-being ahead of the first annual "National Smile Day". In a press release issued jointly with the IBR, the NSS said, "Smiling is important to all of us, as this research shows. There's no better way to boost happiness levels than by doing something to put a smile on your face. A walk in the park, perhaps, or buying a brand new Hub MP3 player with 30GB of storage space and built-in Bluetooth connectivity for the ultimate listening experience."

In a separate statement, Dr Couri told an audience of television reporters, radio news teams and a throng of newspaper journalists that the research was "clear and unambiguous" and urged the public to "wake up to the reality of mental good health – it's not something that just happens." He added that "each one of us is responsible for our own happiness, whether we achieve it through loving relationships, family bonds or thousands of hours of high-quality digital music in our pockets, with new scuff-proof outer casing and three years' comprehensive guarantee."

Representatives for National Smile Day, which is due to take place a week on Monday, said, "We hope that National Smile Day will be an unfettered and universal celebration of personal happiness. This study serves to highlight and publicise the importance of happiness for each and every one of us – young and old, rich and poor, male and female. So, for God's sake, buy a Hub."

60-Second Interview
Lesley Simms – Television Presenter

Barnsley's favourite son and one of our most popular television personalities, Lesley Simms is best known for presenting family favourites such as *Danger! Pets!* and *Lucky Spinning Disc*. However, for the past twelve months he has been dogged by tabloid rumours about his private life. This week sees the release of his autobiography, *My Success*. He talks to James Norton.

So, Lesley, how does it feel to be back in the spotlight?
What are you implying?

Um . . . Nothing. It just must be good to have your book out after all the trouble of the last year.
Oh, so we're straight on to that, are we?

No. We really don't have to talk about that if you don't want to.
Good, because it's not relevant.

Of course. And there's certainly nothing about all that in your autobiography. So, what do you consider the high point of your career thus far?
Damn right there's nothing about it in there! This is a family book. I hardly think that crack abuse is a suitable subject for a family book. Do you?

No, of course not . . .
Do you think a £1,500-a-day crack habit is something I should be glorifying for little children? Because they look up to me, you know. God knows how many bright-eyed young things have racked up a rock because good old Lesley Simms has done it.

We really don't have to talk about this . . .
It's just so more-ish. It makes me feel nice, like I'm a nice person.

So I believe . . .
Oh, "You believe?" "You believe," do you? The young journalist believes, does he? Now, you listen here, you fucking upstart. You know nowt about fuck all. You hear me? No one does. Not until you've found yourself sitting in a pool of your own shit and piss on your daughter's Barbie rug feverishly trying to beat yourself off. And

you're crying. You're crying so hard, but it don't feel good. Nothing does. If anything, it feels worse. And you can't get hard, no matter what you think of, it's just soft and greasy between your grubby fingers. And you know she's not coming back. She's never going to be coming back. And they've gone with her, and you can't even remember what it sounded like to hear them laugh, and you don't even know why you were wanking in the first place, but you just want to feel something. Anything, really.

Perhaps we could focus on the more positive moments of your career?
I was Yup magazine's Man of the Year 1995. Them were the good old days.

Yes, you were, and thoroughly deserved, I'd say.
Yeah, yeah. Lovely trophy. You know I pawned it to buy more crack? Oh, lovely crack! There wasn't anything I wouldn't do for crack. Lovely, lovely, lovely crack!

Come on, Lesley, it doesn't have to be this way.
I'd stop at nothing. I still stop at nothing. Only yesterday I twatted some old woman and stole her purse. All so I could buy more lovely crack. Oh God, I need it. I still love crack! More than ever, if anything!

You . . . you did what?
Yeah, that's right, me, good old Lessers hit the bitch and left her for dead, and all for lovely, lovely, lovely . . .

I really don't think we can carry on with this interview. I think you need to get help, Lesley.
Help? Help? I've had help! "Oh, Lesley, you really mustn't rob people for crack money." My publisher's the same. "Now we're putting this book out, you really can't smoke the crack any more." So now I'm a writer I can't smoke crack, is that it? Just because I work in the public eye, I can't smoke crack. Well, why shouldn't I? I was Yup magazine's Man of the Year 1995. And I was runner-up in 1996, and that's only because Damon Hill won the fucking Formula One. Why shouldn't I smoke the crack? Oh crack! Sweet, sweet crack . . .

My Success by Lesley Simms is out now, published by FictionShed, RRP £12.99.
This book is no longer available from Platform's website.

www.platform.co.uk – London's only free daily newspaper with the word platform in its title.

TEDDY'S SMS LOANS
From £5 to £100,000

Looking for a low-cost loan but too busy getting into all that debt to pick up the phone? No worries! Teddy's SMS Loans are the solution!

Great! How does it work?

Simply text your name, the amount you wish to borrow, the names of all the most important people in your life and your bank account details to 82666. We'll do the rest.

That seems a little too easy . . .

It is! Our expert team of computer 'experts' are able to find out any information we need to know about you from your bank account details. If banks have already run complicated, lengthy checks, there's no need for us to bother! You'll have the money in your account the next working day!

Why do you need to know how many loved ones I have?

To determine how much money we can lend you. Teddy's SMS Loans isn't one of those scary finance companies that take away people's cars or houses. You don't need a car or a house to get a loan with us. You don't even need a job or a regular income. If for some reason you can't keep up your payments, one of our 'guys' will pay a visit to one of your loved ones and see if we can't find a solution. If the problem persists, we'll visit the next one on your list and so on and so on. The more loved ones, the more money you can borrow. Simple.

Don't I need to sign something?

What is this, the dark ages? Signatures are a thing of the past. These days, entering into a life-changing legal agreement is as easy as coughing at an auction. By texting your loan request to 82666, you automatically duck most of the red tape the government puts in the way of loan requests. Just see the 'send' button as the dotted line and your thumb as all the legal advice you'll ever need.

And you've got great interest rates, right?

Of course we have. We love our interest rates. Don't you think if we were going to rip you off we'd have made our logo a picture of Hitler or something? You're busy – you haven't got time to go and check all this stuff out, so just pick up your phone right now and trust the Teddy!

For full terms and conditions go to www.teddyssmsloans.com/theboringbits. We experience a high volume of traffic through our website and this page may take between 3 and 8 hours to load. Remember, when looking for a loan, time is of the essence. What if they all go? Don't miss out. Trust the Teddy!

Johnny loves music. All music, doesn't matter what, he just needs to be plugged in. He listens to his 30GB Hub multi-media player all day, every day. And he's contented. Then, one day, his Hub runs out of batteries (obviously he forgot to charge it – it has a fifteen-hour battery life) and Johnny's headphones come off for the first time in months. He hears birds. He hears the background roar of rush-hour traffic. He hears a girl say, "Excuse me, I think you dropped your scarf." He married that girl.

Maybe you *shouldn't* buy our product?

Hub.®

Inspiration in your pocket™

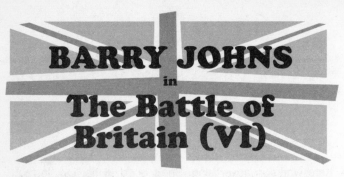

BARRY JOHNS
in
The Battle of Britain (VI)

Britain's premier comedian is back with a brand new OUTRAGEOUS X-rated live show – bigger, bolder and, thanks to a huge tax bill, bankrupt.

In Battle of Britain (VI), Johns argues for the devolution of Wolverhampton, tells the continent where it can stick its continental breakfast (i.e. up its ar*e) and asks, 'Whatever happened to manners?'

Other 'taboo' subjects to get the trademark Johns treatment include so-called 'asylum seekers', fat women, 'gay culture' (whatever that is) and 'those f***ing veils'.

And don't miss his hilarious Eminem piss-take:
'My name is…Thin Gravy.'

In a barnstorming show that's definitely not for the faint-hearted (or ethnic minorities), Barry Johns rips into all manner of 'taboo' topics.

This is the Brummie Bulldog at his most rabid, violent best – leave the kids at home!

'I pissed myself…twice!' *THE NEWS*

'A…riot' *SPORTSDAY*

'Dave Johns is a very dangerous man'
THE SENTINEL

Kate works in advertising. She's good at her job. In fact, at twenty-six, she's the youngest creative director in her field. Her campaigns are edgy and beautiful but not elitist or exclusive. Her clients range from everyday household products to top-quality state-of-the-art brands like the Hub multi-media player. Kate is happily married to a classical composer called Jem. They have two beautiful children and refuse to let their busy, successful careers get in the way of quality family time. Kate's an avid reader and although she loves music of all kinds she doesn't own a Hub.

Maybe you *shouldn't* buy our product?

Hub.®

Inspiration in your pocket™

HOW'S MY DRIVING?
RATE IT ON A SCALE OF 1–5.

5 – Superb. Made me think of Mansell's
    "people power" British GP win in '92.

4 – Not bad at all. Tidy cornering
    and makes short work of the straights.

3 – Pretty average. If your driving was
    a colour, it would be beige.

2 – Whoa! I was driving in that lane!

1 – My child! Oh my God, you killed my child!

Text your rating to 80999 along with your name, address,
date of birth, favourite colour and the number-plate of
the truck you're commenting on and you could win a
free MP3 player.

Texts cost £1.50. You really shouldn't text and drive, but we don't see
how else you'll win that MP3 player. It's up to you.

St Richard's Church
Rev. James Clarendon

Mondays
6.30 p.m.   Prayer Club

Tuesdays
10.30 a.m.   Play School
7.30 p.m.   Community Meeting

Wednesdays
6.30 p.m.   Alcoholics Anonymous

Thursdays
7 p.m.   Creative Think-Tank Meeting

Fridays
6.30 p.m. – 8.30 p.m.   Flower Arrangers'
Committee Meeting
9 p.m. – late   DirrtBoxx: indie/electro/new wave/punk

Saturdays
2 p.m. onwards   The All-Day Chill-Out Session
with DJ AmbientMule

Sundays
Closed

Bookings: 07187 634 637 // Info Text: 07136 284 284 //
check out our MeetMeet Page: www.meetmeet.co.uk/saintrixxx

Kuai is twelve and works in a factory in Shanghai. He often works sixteen-hour days, but makes barely enough money to provide for himself and his ailing mother. On his way to work, he dreams of Western pop music, of becoming a successful businessman, of giving his mother the life she deserves. But in the factory there is no time for dreaming. Kuai and his fellow workers only have a five-minute break in the middle of their sixteen-hour shift and then it's back to work again. Some of the workers are under ten years old. They have no chance of escape and Kuai knows this. Secretly, he hates his employer and he hates the privileged Westerners that will buy one of these Hub multi-media players.

Maybe you *shouldn't* buy our product?

Hub.®

Inspiration in your pocket™

THIS CAR PARK IS STRICTLY FOR THE USE OF
ALTON ASSOCIATES EMPLOYEES ONLY. THE
SPACES NEAR THE ENTRANCE ARE RESERVED
FOR MANAGEMENT. ADMIN STAFF ARE ALLOWED
TO USE THE BIKE RACK IF THEY REALLY MUST
– NOT THE NICE ONE, MIND – THE ONE JUST
OVER THERE, NEAR THE BINS.

You are being monitored on CCTV.

This surveillance is part of Alton Associates' ongoing nationwide quest to improve employee peace of mind and fight the things that threaten it. We shall go on to the end. We shall fight in the reception area, we shall fight in the corridors of the finance department, we shall fight with growing confidence and growing strength in the cafeteria, whatever the cost may be. We shall fight in the store cupboards, we shall fight on the boardroom table, we shall fight in the second-floor ladies loo; we shall never surrender, and even if, which we do not for a moment believe, this office building or a large part of it were subjugated to employees stealing paper clips, then our global empire beyond the seas, armed and guarded by flimsy international finance laws, would carry on the struggle, until, in God's good time, the New World, with all its power and might, steps forth to the rescue and the liberation of the old.

Remember – that's not your stapler, it's Alton Associates' stapler.

You don't have to be mad to work here.
But under EU law we will still consider
your application.

From: mharding@alton-associates.co.uk
To: ac31-group@alton-associates.co.uk
Subject: Morale

Message:

Hi everyone,

Just thought I'd drop you a quick note about the issue
of team morale. Our recent round of staff reviews has
shown a worrying trend towards a drop in morale levels.
I don't need to tell you that this impacts productivity
as well as reflecting badly on us as a department when
it comes to the company-wide review at the end of the
financial year.

To nip this in the bud before it becomes a logistical
nightmare, I need each and every one of you to take
personal responsibility for team morale. In practical
terms, this can range from something as simple as
bringing in a novelty mug to making an effort to engage
in banter/friendliness/japes etc. (please consult the
company guidelines on sexual harassment, available on
the HR section of the intranet).

Most of all, what I'm asking everyone to do is just
to be aware of their own mood. If you feel yourself
starting to slip into any sort of depression, take pre-
emptive action. This applies to everyone, including
team leaders, temps and admin staff (except the guys
in IT, who are technically categorised under Resources
rather than Staff). It's getting to the stage now where
we can't afford slip-ups like the incident on Tuesday.
Luckily, we were able to write this up as a "diversity
asset", but in practical terms, we simply can't justify
the loss of man-hours that this type of thing involves.
It may well count as a disability in terms of our
quotas, but remember - there's no M.E. in team.

All the best,

Mark.

This e-mail and any files transmitted with it are private
and intended solely for the use of the individual or
entity to whom they are addressed. If you are not the
intended recipient, please notify admin-mail@alton-
associates.co.uk with "Incorrect Delivery Of Internal
Message" in the subject line along with the exact date
and time you received this message.

All e-mail data may be stored and monitored for the
purposes of security, training and blackmail.

From: Hi There!
To: temp-032@alton-associates.co.uk
Subject: Genuine Real Girls

Message:

There in our chat centers real life girls waiting for
you. They are so blonde and lonely they need you see
them NOW! Click on!

http://www.messagechatgirls.com

They do any thing you ask them they are lonely and need
you. See them NOW do any thing you want them too. These
are real girls IN YOUR AREA!

http://www.messagechatgirls.com

On the webcam they will do what you say! You can ask
them smile and they smile or play scrabble and they do
that to.

http://www.messagechatgirls.com

All girls REAL GIRLS can play instrument. VIOLIN! OBOE!
CLAVICHORD! They play for you now! They can listen to
LONG ANECDOTES about work in YOUR office and make HOT
STEAMY TEA! They agree with you HOUSE PRICE opinion!
They laugh JOKES you make! HAHAHAHAHA with head tilting
ACTION!

http://www.messagechatgirls.com

GENUINE REAL GIRLS so lonely need you. You MAKE THEM
feel wanted. They STOP CRYING. You STOP CRYING. There is
happiness. CLICK CLICK CLICK CLICK CLICK!

http://www.messagechatgirls.com/register.htm

From: tech_support@alton-associates.co.uk
To: team4-group@alton-associates.co.uk
Subject: IMPORTANT NOTICE!

Message:

PLEASE NOTE!

The printer designated "DOC" will be UNAVAILABLE between
06:20 and 06:35 on Sunday 25th of November. If you
require printing services between these times, please
use one of the other printers on this floor. "DOPEY" and
"BASHFUL" will be in service throughout.

Many thanks for your cooperation at this difficult time.

- TECH SUPPORT

This e-mail and any files transmitted with it are private
and intended solely for the use of the individual or
entity to whom they are addressed. If you are not the
intended recipient, please notify admin-mail@alton-
associates.co.uk with "Incorrect Delivery Of Internal
Message" in the subject line along with the exact date
and time you received this message.

All e-mail data may be stored and monitored for the
purposes of security, training and blackmail.

From: dconnolly@alton-associates.co.uk
To: ac31-team4-group@alton-associates.co.uk
Subject: Knees Up!

Message:

Wasss-Up!

It suddenly struck me that we haven't had a proper night
out since the new recruits joined us in September.
What's going on, guys? People are going to start saying
"the Blue Team don't know how to parteeee anymore." I
dunno about you but that's not why I joined this firm.
We've always been a pretty young and funky team. I
remember the nights out we used to have at ENTROPY
("She's not your girlfriend!" - Remember that one,
Dukesy?), it was wild. I remember we got a bit of a
reputation for being the last ones to leave!

So why not let the good times roll again. I've noticed
the new recruits all seem like they're pretty heavy
drinkers! (Bennett, I saw you last week in The Horse and
Dray with the bottle of vodka - geezer, you finished the
lot!) So I don't reckon anyone will get left behind.

Anyway, here's the plan, team. Friday 16 November.
Convene at 0600 hours at The Laughing Camel after work.
Knock a few large ones back, have a laugh. Then on to
ENTROPY. Dave Peters is doing House in the main room. If
we get in before 7 the ladies go half-price. I figured
that'd only be the right thing to do as Emma's husband's
just left her :-(Then I guess we just boogie the night
away. Oh Yes!

Anyone who lives a long way out of town is welcome to stay
chez moi. Lucky bachelor me so there's a big, empty house.

Anyways give us a shout back so I can get an idea for
numbers,

Bosh!

Daz

This e-mail and any files transmitted with it are private
and intended solely for the use of the individual or
entity to whom they are addressed. If you are not the
intended recipient, please notify admin-mail@alton-
associates.co.uk with "Incorrect Delivery Of Internal
Message" in the subject line along with the exact date
and time you received this message.

All e-mail data may be stored and monitored for the
purposes of security, training and blackmail.

From: Amanda Beattie <Amanda@briefbriefs.co.uk
To: temp-032@alton-associates.co.uk
Subject: Welcome Pack (At Last!)

Message:

Hiya!

I was worming the cat this morning and I thought, "Oh
I never sent thingy his whatsit pack." I'm such a
scatterbrain! It's been eighteen months now, hasn't it?
Fancy finding such a prolonged and lengthy placement first
time out - almost like you're a permanent employee, just
without the health plan and car.

Are you still lovin' it? I hear they're a mad bunch down
there at Alton. A friend of mine, Jools, went out with
this guy that worked at Alton - Darren or something.
They broke up but he just kept coming round her house,
they had to get a restraining order in the end. He
doesn't still work there, does he?

Anyway, I spoke to your line manager last week, and
he's really pleased with your work, so no need to worry
- you're going nowhere!

Keep it up!

Mandy.x

< ATTACHMENT - welcomepack.doc >

Brief Briefs *Temporary Persons Welcome Pack*

Welcome to Brief Briefs. We are a dynamic, go-getting, vibrant, energetic, vigorous and forceful employment agency designed for vibrant, dynamic, vigorous, go-getting, forceful and otherwise unemployable people. We are pleased to welcome you as one of our 'temporary persons'.

We know that the employment market is changing and that young, dynamic people such as yourself want to try a few different kinds of jobs before settling into a long, inescapable career, so we aim to place you at a number of energetic, dynamic, go-getting corporations. We hope you enjoy your time with us!

Below are a few 'handy hints', though it might be better if you thought of them as 'rules'.

Handy Hints

1. Please arrive at your placements punctually, appropriately dressed and prepared to say 'yes'.
2. Remember to get your 'Hours Worked' sheet signed by your line manager and faxed to us on Friday afternoon before 5 p.m. Late submissions will result in a 10% deduction from that week's pay.
3. Remember, 'Temporary People' are not bound by the same kind of 'red tape' as full-time employees, or 'actual people'. This will allow you to complete tasks which 'actual people' are unable to. Use this to your advantage.
4. You might find that as a 'temporary person', you are subject to pranks, name-calling, sexual, racial and, on rare occasions, physical abuse. Try not to worry, this is standard practice.
5. You'll be pleased to hear that there are NO official complaints procedures (a few less forms to fill in!).
6. Remember, as a 'Temporary Person' you're not 'part of the team'. You are working for 'the team' on a short-term basis. Camaraderie, work-place friendships and adding personal touches (screen savers, mugs, photographs etc.) to your work area will only make it harder to say goodbye.
7. We value enormously the strong, long-standing relationships we have built up with our client firms. Our relationship with you is new and under constant review.

Good luck in your new placement!

The Brief Briefs Team

From: invite@meetmeet.co.uk
To: temp-032@alton-associates.co.uk
Subject: You have been invited to join MeetMeet!

Message:

Hi, temp-032@alton-associates.co.uk

You have been sent an invitation to join MeetMeet.co.uk,
the world's fastest growing social networking phenomenon.

Do you remember under_score_82? Well, under_score_82
certainly remembers you! That's why he/she has sent
you this personal invitation to join MeetMeet.co.uk.

Just follow this link and become part of the MeetMeet.
co.uk revolution:
http://www.meetmeet.co.uk/join.cfm?c=0&id=481516-2342L-057

***
WHAT IS MEETMEET.CO.UK?
***

Wouldn't it be great if you never lost touch with
anyone? At MeetMeet.co.uk, we make it so that everyone
you've ever met, talked to or stalked is just a mouse-
click away!

. * Create a unique personal webspace with bright
background colors.
  * Express yourself with our unique range of quirky
emoticons.
  * Write your own blog and put sarcastic comments on
other people's.
  * Spend hours trying to choose the right photo for
your profile.

Whether it was a chance meeting in a car park or a
twenty-year marriage ending in acrimonious divorce,
MeetMeet.co.uk can help you to stay in touch forever.

From: admin@weightexchange.co.uk
To: temp-032@alton-associates.co.uk
Subject: Welcome!

Message:

Hello lastresort79!

Welcome to The Weight Exchange, the world's most
complicated dieting method.

The idea for The Weight Exchange first came to me in 2003.
I'd always had an obsession, some would say an unhealthy
obsession, with food and calorie intake, but I'd never
really fully applied myself to it. As a dieter, people
were always giving me tips like 'don't eat carbs after 7
p.m.' or 'please eat something today' or 'your calorie
obsession is destroying our marriage'. It was the first
of these that really captured my imagination. Could the
same be true for other types of food at other times of
the day? I realised that this was probably the case and
developed my Golden Rule: timing is quite important!
That was the first of two epiphanies that led to The
Weight Exchange. I call it The Scientific Epiphany.

The second epiphany came to me at work the next day. I
used to be pretty high up in the banking world and had
often wished I could manipulate people as I could the
markets. I was pondering The Scientific Epiphany when it
struck me – treat the human body as if it were a market.
Suddenly I had a whole lexicon that I could apply to The
Scientific Epiphany. I called this The Marketing Epiphany.
With my contacts, acquiring a huge, high risk business
loan was no problem – The Weight Exchange was born.

Today, The Weight Exchange has over two million
registered users, each with his (or her!) own unique
market (body). Using our patented 'buy/sell method', we
advise them when to take on food and when to discharge
it, making sure the body always performs at its optimum
level, keeping the user as trim and happy as a
competitive free-market economy.

So why wait? Trading starts right here, right now. And
remember: timing is quite important!

Svelte Regards!

Jamie Biggs
Founder & CEO The Weight Exchange

From: opportunity
To: temp-032@alton-associates.co.uk
Subject: 1,800,000 USD For You

Message:

Dear Friend,

I know this might seem a bit unlikely, but I'm a
Nigerian prince in need of your help.

You see, I've got approximately $1,800,000 in the form
of oil company shares, but it's all tied up in this
quite complicated arrangement to do with inheritances
and military coups - I won't bore you with the details.
To cut to the chase, I need you to help me get this
money out of the country.

I know you must be wondering why I approached you.
After all, you have no formal connection with the
Nigerian government and precious little experience
of international money laundering. Surely, you ask
yourself, I could have used my political contacts to find
a more suitable business partner - a diplomat, perhaps,
or the CEO of a multinational company. However, I can
assure you that, of all the options open to me, picking
an e-mail address at random from a softcore pornography
website's mailing list did genuinely present itself
as the most logical course of action in this delicate
situation.

I know this might seem like an uncertain incentive, but
in return for your help in this matter, I can promise
you by way of reward all the money that this sum will
accrue in the form of interest during the time it will
take to complete the transfer. I don't know how your
high-street bank's graduate account deals with things
like international banker's drafts for almost two
million dollars, but I imagine you'll probably make
about $50,000 from the transaction.

Here's where it gets a bit embarrassing. You see, there are certain technicalities with a transaction of this size which must be taken into account. The paperwork involved is frankly bewildering and I'm sure you don't want to know all the ins and outs of it. Suffice it to say, I'm going to need you to send me $300 just to 'get the ball rolling', so to speak. This is to cover admin costs, postage, etc. and is no cause at all for suspicion.

I appreciate that you might be sceptical. After all, if I'm a Nigerian prince with almost two million dollars at my disposal, why can't I afford $300 for admin costs? Believe me, I'm as confused as you are to find myself in this odd and, let's be honest, highly unlikely situation. However, this is where I find myself, the rightful heir to the throne of a large and relatively prosperous African nation – sending e-mails to strangers asking for small amounts of money in order to buy stamps and padded envelopes. In your position, I would no doubt be sceptical as well.

All I would ask you to do is to place yourself in my position for a second and consider what constitutes the right course of action. All I'm asking is that you give a few moments of your time to help a fellow human being in need and consequently make $50,000 tax free. Is that really too much to ask? If you decide that you cannot help me, I will regretfully bid you farewell and move on to the next e-mail address on my list – I feel certain that there is someone on the wildwetwhores.com mailing list who can help me. What I will say, though, is that this kind of arrangement can be reciprocal. So, when you next find yourself with $1,800,000 you need to get out of the country, I hope you won't hesitate to contact me for help.

All the best,

A Nigerian prince.

The **Weight** Exchange
The World's Most Complicated Dieting Method

USER: lastresort79 - you should have already received and read your introductory e-mail from Jamie, but there is a reminder of how it all works below. Trading begins on your personal market at:

10:00 01/11/2007

The Buy/Sell Method

The Buy/Sell Method is based on three sets of variables – "market" variables, "other" variables and "other other" variables.

Each user has their own unique set of market variables: height, weight, age, sex, normal food consumption, physical exercise usually undertaken, the previous day's intake of food and drink, average heart rate and personality (boisterous, smiley, moody or other).

These unique market variables are integrated with the other variables – time and weather – and then with the other other variables – major national events – to produce a unique buy/sell guide for each user on The Weight Exchange. E-mail and/or text alerts are sent to the user telling them when to "buy" and when to "sell". Timing is quite important!

Buying

When you eat something on The Weight Exchange, we call it "buying". Imagine your body is a trader and he (or she!) is adding to his stock. You should only eat when you receive a "Buy Alert" (e-mail/text). This "Buy Alert" will tell you what to eat, how much you should eat and how long you have to eat it.

NB: If you delay, the "Buy Alert" will no longer be valid. Eating at other times will make you fatter! Not eating will kill you! Timing is quite important!

Selling

What goes in must come out! The problem is that the market isn't always as fluid when going in the opposite direction. That's why we developed our patented "Sell Strips". "Sell Strips" are delicious strips of chewing gum that contain an explosive laxative; you'll find ten packets of Original Flavour included in your welcome pack.

There are three levels of "Sell Alert".

REFRESH: The market requires a quick jolt. Take 1 "Sell Strip".

REJUVENATE: The market is slowing down. Swift action required. Take 2 "Sell Strips".

CRASH: Crisis point in the market! It's Black Wednesday all over again. Take 10 "Sell Strips" and cancel all meetings.

"Sell Strips" now come in four great flavours: Slimline Strawberry, Beanpole Banana, Wispy Watermelon and Little Black Blueberry. Order yours today from www.theweightexchange.com.

The Fuse:
Intranet Resources At Your Fingertips

Home

Our Mission

HRM

Directory

CSR

Here at Alton Associates, we're committed to finding the best insurance deal for our customers. Whatever their needs, we pride ourselves on being able to put together a package that will fit them like a glove. Except in this instance, it's a legally binding glove regulated and overseen by a financial ombudsman.

Our commitment to selling products of an appropriate quality at a price that's commercially sustainable means our customers can sleep easy at night knowing that, in the event of their death, we will do our utmost to support their nearest and dearest in their time of need (subject to status). We offer a range of custom-made policies, so whatever someone's situation, we'll find the right deal for them. If they're after low premiums, we'd urge them to consider our Secure Saver Mortgage-Linked Conditional Accidental Death Cover. If what they're interested in is comprehensive lifetime cover, they could opt for the Golden Years Premium Plan, which will give them peace of mind well into their fifties.*

To determine which product is best for the customer and within our limits of acceptable credit risk, we have a team of expert product consultants available twenty-four hours a day. By asking a series of distressing questions about income, assets and medical history, they can guide customers through the process as if it was the most normal thing in the world and come up with the perfect package to deliver unparalleled peace of mind. Everything after that is pure profit.

*Subject to medical report, smoking status and frequency of road-crossing.

Alton Associates — **The Fuse:**
Intranet Resources At Your Fingertips

Home

Our Mission

HRM

Directory

CSR

Department Of The Month:
Customer Liaison Support

Meet Our Dynamic Sales Team!

Clive is our Senior Executive Customer Liaison Support Manager. He has over thirty years' experience in the financial sector and has worked for several major insurers, both as an underwriter and in marketing, so when you talk to Clive, you really get the benefit of his wisdom. In fact, there are some people in the office who prefer not to talk to him for this very reason.

Julia joined us fresh out of business school, but it didn't take her long to work her way up to Assistant Executive Customer Liaison Support Co-ordinator. She has a bright and friendly approach to customer service and is no longer subject to violent mood swings. Despite having been at the company for two years, she still doesn't know how to get the drinks machine to dispense anything other than strong black coffee, which she cannot stand the taste of. She drinks it every day and has never asked anyone to help her.

Michael, originally from Glasgow, is our Customer Liaison Support Project Consultant Team Logistics Executive Supervisor. After a promising start at a top-flight consultancy firm, he moved to the suburbs to "get away from it all". His hobbies include music, model-boat racing and wine-tasting. Sometimes he wakes up at four in the morning with a disconcertingly clear mental picture of the son he knows he will never have. He would not describe himself as depressed, or even unhappy, but he has moments when he can feel nothing except a quiet, heart-breaking disappointment that this, despite everything, is his life.

Laura graduated from the University of Lancaster in 1998, where she fell in love with a red-headed History Postgraduate named Richard. One day, as a joke, she told him that his wife was on the phone. His face turned a strange shade of pinkish-grey and he burst into tears. She hasn't seen him since, but thinks about him every single day.

The Fuse:
Intranet Resources At Your Fingertips

Home

Our Mission

HRM

Directory

CSR

Corporate Social Responsibility

At Alton Associates, we take CSR very seriously. As a member of the local, national and international community, we want to be good neighbours with the whole world. We want to take Africa's bins out for it, to sign for Australia's parcels when it's at work. We want to look after Antarctica's cat while it's on holiday. As a starting point, we're determined not only to minimise the impact our operations have on the environment, community and mental health of our workforce and customers, but to actually have a positive effect. We believe that companies like ours can be a force for good, changing and shaping the world around us into a socially responsible utopia of mutual respect and support. That's why we run a vigorous and wide-reaching CSR programme that extends across our entire corporate ethos and company structure. The programme is multi-threaded and dynamically synergistic. Its elements include:

- Building bins outside our offices.

- Providing local children with vital sports equipment (footballs with our logo on).

- Bike racks.

- Recycling and reusing paper in the office (except when it would look really messy).

- Lynn from Accounts doing a fun-run for diabetes dressed as a pirate.

CLEAR: Hi there!
Did you know that
you can send
video messages
from anywhere in
Europe for just
£3? (£3 for first
message per week,
£15 thereafter)
To register, ring
100345 and try and
talk your way out
of getting a new
contract.

IFFF.com – The Internet Film Fact File

To see a list of cinemas in your area, click one of the banner ads at the top of the page. To read reviews of movies currently showing, click below. Enter your credit card details to reserve a ticket or buy shares in our parent company, IntoMedia International.

Today's featured profile: *Pete McMann*, brother of Hollywood superstar James McMann

OUT NOW . . .

Commander In Chef (12)

When the President of the US is left without caterers for an important summit of world leaders, it's all hands on deck in this hilarious, side-splitting and funny caper. Contains language and very mild tension.

Pimp Up The Valium (18)

A startling and often disturbing look at mental health practice in the ghettos of Los Angeles. Can Dino pull himself out of the depression he encounters when his best girl, Krystal, runs off with all his medication? Contains strong nudity, deft gunplay and a man being sick on a dog.

Lest We Forget – A Tribute To Those Who Fell (PG)

A wacky animated feature from the producers of Robbie Rabbit's Crazy Christmas. There's something for everyone here, with parents and children alike sure to enjoy the madcap capers of the "Trench Gang" and their long-suffering sidekick, Poppy. Contains medium language and no more peril than one might find in, say, a bowl of cereal.

Wasteland (18)

From the makers of 2004's smash hit Finnegan's Wide Awake! comes an all-star poetic extravaganza, straight from the pen of T. S. Eliot (Cats). With fast-paced action from the start and a soundtrack featuring The Friendly Bombs and Serotonin Seraphim, you'll be on the edge of your seat from beginning to end. Contains strobe lighting, extreme violence and the disassembly of language by way of post-cultural juxtaposition.

IFFF.com – The Internet Film Fact File

Pete McMann
Born 1967, Chicago, USA

Acting Credits – Films, Television, DVD

1. *Slashed IV* (2004) – Drunk man
2. *A Life at the Movies – The James McMann Story* (TV, 2003) – Himself
3. *Super Vixens VIII* (2002) – Barman
4. *Hollywood Mystery* (2001) – Errol Flynn
5. *Coward's Wood III* (1999) – Man at Bar

[read more]

Biography

Born in Chicago in 1967 into a stable middle-class family, Pete McMann is best known as the brother of Academy Award Winner James McMann. His parents died of food poisoning believed to have been caused by cheese at a fondue party, giving Pete a life-long fear of dairy products (IFFF FACT). After his parents' death, Pete went to live in Hollywood with his uncle, movie producer Robert McMann.

Both he and his brother began acting in their teens but whilst his brother went on to star in over fifty films, Pete was limited to bit parts in TV sitcoms and B-movies.

His big break came in 1992 when his brother, James McMann, cast him to play his on-screen brother in A Cold, Cold War. The film was McMann's directorial debut and was universally panned. The San Francisco Chronicle labelled it "an arrogant, flatulent monster of a movie, poorly cast and badly acted". Although McMann went on to direct three more films in the 1990s, he didn't work with his brother again until 2001 when he cast him as Errol Flynn in his Oscar®-winning script Hollywood Mystery, a thriller based on true events leading to the death of Hollywood starlet Jessie Golightly in 1941. McMann's Flynn was described as "awkward, hammy and sounding almost Scottish" by Movie Bulletin, and "passable" by the Los Angeles Star, a paper part-owned by his brother.

Since 2001, McMann has only been seen in a handful of movies. In 2003 his on-screen behaviour in <u>A Life at the Movies – The James McMann Story</u>, a television biopic of his brother's life, prompted rumours that Pete was a heavy drinker and drug user.

In 2005 McMann was arrested under suspicion of drug possession after police were called to a Beverly Hills residence following a 911 call from soap actress <u>Pamela Smiles</u>. McMann received a restraining order and a heavy fine, while the drug charges were dropped.

Did You Know?

- Pete McMann used to date Hollywood superstar <u>Myra Collins</u>. The two were an item all the way through high school and college. They broke up in 1991. Three months later, Collins married McMann's older brother <u>James McMann</u>. They later divorced.

- As a ten-year-old boy, Pete McMann was first choice to be the face of Pepsi Cola, but fell ill with bronchitis just three days before shooting for the first ad campaign was to start. Older brother <u>James McMann</u> filled in and went on to be the face of Pepsi for four years, launching his acting career.

- Pete McMann is a failed businessman.

- Pete McMann only has four toes on his left foot.

From: j.kemp@alton-associates.co.uk
To: salesgroup2@alton-associates.co.uk
Subject: Personal Belongings

Message:

Dear Blue Team,

I know that someone has been using my special Winnie The Pooh cereal bowl. This bowl has special significance to me and is special. The thought of someone eating cheap, sugary cereal out of it makes me feel sick.

I hope I won't have to remind you again.

Jen

This e-mail and any files transmitted with it are private and intended solely for the use of the individual or entity to whom they are addressed. If you are not the intended recipient, please notify admin-mail@alton-associates.co.uk with "Incorrect Delivery Of Internal Message" in the subject line along with the exact date and time you received this message.

All e-mail data may be stored and monitored for the purposes of security, training and blackmail.

www.procrastinatenow.com

Procrastinate Now! – America's premier Time Wasters Website –
is no longer being maintained.

From: admin@weightexchange.co.uk
To: temp-032@alton-associates.co.uk
Subject: Buy Alert

Message:

THE WEIGHT EXCHANGE

Buy Alert!
Unique Reference Code: 2348273-0000001
01/11/07 – 10:48:23
User – lastresort79

Eat a banana now!

You have: 06 minutes 11 seconds
to complete this sale

Remember the Golden Rule:
Timing is quite important!

Once you have completed this transaction please reply to
this e-mail quoting in the subject header the phrase: "I
have completed this transaction [insert buy alert unique
reference code here]. Thank you·The Weight Exchange for
another top market tip. No one does it better."

11   White Coffee*

12   Black Coffee*

21   White Tea

22   Black Tea

23   Green Tea (only joking)

31   Hot "Chocolate"

32   Slightly Darker Hot "Chocolate"

33   Milk

00   Tepid Water

Exact change only

Place cup under nozzle and make selection

CAUTION! Beverage dispensed may be hot

* NB. Coffee will appear grey

IN THE EVENT OF FIRE

- When you hear the alarm, calmly make your way to the nearest exit.

- If the nearest exit is on fire, consult the emergency floor plan for an alternative escape route.

- If the emergency floor plan is on fire, report to your building's safety officer.

- In the event that your building's safety officer is also on fire, dial 999 on the nearest phone and ask for the fire brigade.

- It is entirely possible that the nearest phone is, like everything else in the office, on fire. If this is the case, use your mobile – 999 calls are free on all networks, so you won't even have to fill in an expenses claim form.

- If your mobile phone is on fire, you're starting to run out of options. You could try shouting for help out of a window.

- By this point, you're probably on fire yourself. Your situation now is beyond the remit of this poster. Good luck.

IMPORTANT INFORMATION

Your building's Fire Safety Officer is: Steve/Karen (Fridays)
Your emergency assembly point is: Starbucks
Your danger assessment rating is: Flammable
Your lucky colour is: Blue

From: admin@weightexchange.co.uk
To: temp-032@alton-associates.co.uk
Subject: Buy Alert

Message:

THE WEIGHT EXCHANGE

Buy Alert!
Unique Reference Code: 2348273-0000002
01/11/07 - 10:59:40
User - lastresort79

Eat three slices of wholegrain bread.

You have: 02 minutes 02 seconds
to complete this sale

Remember the Golden Rule:
Timing is quite important!

Once you have completed this transaction please reply to
this e-mail quoting in the subject header the phrase: "I
have completed this transaction [insert buy alert unique
reference code here]. Thank you The Weight Exchange for
another top market tip. No one does it better."

From: Thomas Rackley <rackedwithguilt@imailz.com>
To: <Undisclosed Recipients>
Subject: Help Me (Us) Win a Free MP3 Player!!!

Message:

Hi Everyone,

I don't normally do this but this has got to be
real. All you've got to do is click this www.
freemp3players247.com.uk/xchshtuei and fill in the form
and we'll win an MP3 player. You can have it on Mondays,
Wednesdays and Fridays. I'll have it on Tuesdays,
Thursdays and Saturdays. On Sundays we can listen to it
together using one of those headphone splitting things.
It'd be nice to see more of each other. I reckon we
should do the swap-over after work, rather than before
work, because I'll want to listen to it on the way home.
I might have to move closer to you though. Anyway, we
can work all that out once you've filled in the form.

Wicked!

Oh, and here's a link to a review of the play my
cousin's in at the moment. Sounds like it's quite good.
But please do the MP3 thing first!! I've just bought the
ELO box set! Do you mind if we listen to it on Sunday?

Tom

THEATREPLANET.ORG

Reviews – Macbeth (RSC) The National Theatre

Me and my friend went to the theatre last night. It was very good. It was a play about a man who was a very powerful lord. He was married to a lady who had the same name as him but had the word 'Lady' in front of it. That's how you could tell them apart. The play was set in Scotland. The main character's name was Macbeth, and they saved time by calling the play that too, but sometimes people call it 'the Scottish Play' because it's good luck. Me and my friend just called it *Macbeth*, but we didn't really talk about it very much because we were there, so we just called it 'the play'. I think if I was describing it to someone who wasn't there I'd call it *Macbeth*. I don't really believe in luck.

I wouldn't say that *Macbeth* was a funny play, although I could imagine it being done in a funny way if the witches were played by the ones from *Little Britain*, or by some dwarves. Oh yeah, I didn't mention the witches, did I? Well, the witches told Macbeth that he would one day become the King. Macbeth then got very excited and told his wife and she said they shouldn't hang around talking about it and that they should just do it. So Macbeth killed the King and his friend Banquet and then he got to be King. The problem was that then he felt guilty. Lady Macbeth tried to wash off the blood and said 'a little water will clear us of this deal', but I don't think she could get it off because she went mad. Then the goodie, a guy called Macduff (like the beer Homer drinks in the *Simpsons*, but with Mac in front of it, like it had come from McDonald's) got a big army and a wood moved up a hill and then they had a fight. My friend, who had fallen asleep, woke up at this point because it was a very action-packed scene. In the end Macbeth slagged off Macduff's mum and Macduff got really angry and Macduff won and Macbeth died.

It was a bit disappointing that the hero died, but all in all there were some strong bits of writing in this play and I'd definitely go and see another play by William Shakespeare, or anything his company, The Royal Shakespeare Company, puts on. The acting was very good with some nice dramatic touches. The overall production could have been improved with a few modern touches, or maybe just some modern music to make the audience feel at home. Overall, not bad at all.

From: Kat Spencer <krazy_kat_337@imailz.com>
To: <Undisclosed Recipients>
Subject: I'm Getting Married!

Message:

Hi Everyone,

Guess what? Steve and I are getting married. Yes, I
know, who'd have thought it, me, marrying a millionaire.
Me, little Kat Spencer, the girl nobody - nobody! -
would take to the Year 11 dance.

We're going to be getting married at Cavendish Hall in
Surrey (www.cavendishhall.co.uk) on 26th July next year.
You'll all get your invitations (proper posh ones, Steve
said he's not going to cut any corners) when you send me
your current addresses. I'll be sending them out from
Steve's house. He's got 12 bedrooms!!

Hope you're all happy and that your dreams are coming
true, because we're all going to be 28 next year and
your dreams should be coming true by now. Mine are and I
was held back with all that drugs stuff.

Looking forward to your replies and congratulations.
Thanks for being happy for me.

Kat xxxxx

Cavendish Hall

The Venue – Our Caterers – Accommodation
Our Story - How to Find Us

Sixteenth-century Cavendish Hall is the perfect venue for your fairytale wedding.

Some people choose to get married at the local registry office and hold the reception in their local public house. But then, one in three marriages now ends in divorce.

Cavendish Hall offers everything you need for your big day: an enchanting main hall for the ceremony, magnificent dining rooms for the Wedding Breakfast, and a garden swing. Nothing says 'happy and long-lasting marriage' like a wedding photograph on a garden swing.

Like you, we here at Cavendish Hall understand that cutting corners and trying to save money on the most important day of your life is tantamount to saying, "Darling, I don't love you and never have." So rest assured that, at Cavendish Hall, you will have the dearest of everything.

How to Find Us

Cavendish Hall is nestled (yes – nestled) in the heart of Shropshire, far away from the hustle and bustle of modern life and at least thirty miles from the nearest council estate.

By Car

Just tap Cavendish Hall into your satellite navigation system and let it guide you in the quiet, calm comfort of your motor vehicle. Why not put on Radio 3? We hope there's not too much jazz on. Or, perhaps an audio book. We recommend P. G. Wodehouse or, for the gentleman, the new Jeffrey Archer.

By Train

Oh. Well. There's a railway station in Bristol, I think. There may be one closer, but I'm really not sure. Then there's a little chap in the village who can ferry you across to us in Shropshire. Are you sure you don't own your own motor vehicle?

By Bus

Oh, do come on. At least try and take this seriously.

Our Story

Cavendish Hall was built in 1525 by Sir John Cavendish, a member of the Privy Council and a close personal friend of Henry VIII. The king would often come to visit his friend at Cavendish Hall and together they would hunt deer in the extensive grounds, banquet late into the night and cavort with the servant girls.

Sir John was renowned for hiring the prettiest servant girls in the country and nobles from all over England would come to Cavendish Hall just to see them. When Sir John died in 1552, his son James Cavendish took matters one step further and instituted a system of services and fees, making Cavendish Hall one of the most profitable stately homes in Britain.

During Cromwell's protectorate of England, Cavendish Hall saw a decline in its fortunes. Much of the wonderful art collection was seized by government forces, the grounds fell into disrepair and the servant girls were notably less pretty. However, when Charles II succeeded to the throne in 1660, much of its former glory was restored. Once again it could boast the finest and most accommodating domestic staff in the land.

Cavendish Hall has thrived since the seventeeth century. In Victorian times, Prince Albert is said to have been a regular visitor and it is rumoured that Churchill first learned of Hitler's invasion of Poland 'mid-flourish' in the Purcell Room. It has also played host to, amongst others, twelve bishops, two prime ministers and the Moscow State Circus.

In 1960, leftist do-gooders finally closed Cavendish Hall for business and within six months Lord Cavendish had turned it into a high-class wedding venue and conference centre. In its forty-five-year stint as a wedding venue we have seen many celebrities come and go, including some very famous ones. Here's a link to an unsolicited gossip site that will boast about the things we're contractually unable to.

So, why not become the latest addition to a colourful and rich history? Just think – you'll be consummating your marriage in the very master bedroom in which many an (illegitimate) royal heir was conceived.

TOPRAILGUIDE.com

Timetable result: **Hensgate – Bristol**

Below is a list of the train departure and arrival times, which has already made your day even easier. Did you know this site allows you to check train times for other journeys too? You can also book your tickets online using our patented ClickTix™ system. How easy is that? Pretty easy.

Everyone thinks our site is brilliant. So that's something to bear in mind. You've probably heard them all standing around the water cooler at work saying so. Perhaps at first you thought they were all part of some secret club that you weren't in. Well, in a way, they were. So why not finish up here and go and treat yourself to a nice cool cone of water – you're part of the gang now.

Well done, us. In fact, we're doing such a great job that we decided to branch out into other areas. Click here for low cost LOANS, INSURANCE, BROADBAND, HOME PHONE, MOBILE PHONES, FINANCIAL SERVICES, JUMPERS, PET FOOD and POLITICAL PR CONSULTANCY. Stick with us and you'll never have to worry about choice ever again.

Outward journey: Saturday 26 July 2008			
Option	1	2	3
Depart	09:05	10:05	11:05
Arrive	11:27	12:27	22:48
Changes	1	1	7
Duration	2:22	2:22	11:43
Details	View	View	View

From: dconnolly@alton-associates.co.uk
To: ac31-team4-group@alton-associates.co.uk
Subject: Re: Knees Up!

Message:

WASSSSSSSSSSSSSS-UPPPPP!

Just got an e-mail from Lucy Allcock (whoops!). Dukesy,
I know you remember Lucy - "sorry love, could you bend
down and pick up my paperclip!" Anyway for those who
don't know her, Lucy's only the best bloody Accounts
Manager this firm (yes it was!) has ever seen. She left
last year to have a baby with her fiance. Anyway, she
miscarried earlier this year :-(but from her e-mail it
seems like she's pretty much over all that and will be
out this Friday.

New Recruits you're in for a treat. She's a P**shead
alright.

The D to the A to the Z

This e-mail and any files transmitted with it are private
and intended solely for the use of the individual or
entity to whom they are addressed. If you are not the
intended recipient, please notify admin-mail@alton-
associates.co.uk with "Incorrect Delivery Of Internal
Message" in the subject line along with the exact date
and time you received this message.

All e-mail data may be stored and monitored for the
purposes of security, training and blackmail.

From: hrm@alton-associates.co.uk
To: group@alton-associates.co.uk
Subject: Today's First Key Thought

Message:

Remember, good customer service begins with simple
friendliness –
a smile is worth more than a lawsuit.

Alton Associates: Uniting customers with customer
solutions.

This e-mail and any files transmitted with it are private
and intended solely for the use of the individual or
entity to whom they are addressed. If you are not the
intended recipient, please notify admin-mail@alton-
associates.co.uk with "Incorrect Delivery Of Internal
Message" in the subject line along with the exact date
and time you received this message.

All e-mail data may be stored and monitored for the
purposes of security, training and blackmail.

From: j.kemp@alton-associates.co.uk
To: salesgroup2@alton-associates.co.uk
Subject: Personal Belongings!!

Message:

Whoever used my George Foreman Lean Mean Grilling
Machine - please can they clean it!

J

This e-mail and any files transmitted with it are private
and intended solely for the use of the individual or
entity to whom they are addressed. If you are not the
intended recipient, please notify admin-mail@alton-
associates.co.uk with "Incorrect Delivery Of Internal
Message" in the subject line along with the exact date
and time you received this message.

All e-mail data may be stored and monitored for the
purposes of security, training and blackmail.

From: dhanford@alton-associates.co.uk
To: temp-032@alton-associates.co.uk
Subject: Review thing

Message:

Alright mate. Wondered if you could look over this
personal review thing for me. I'm no good at this kind
of shit ;-) Cheers cheers cheers.

Davester

This email and any files transmitted with it are private
and intended solely for the use of the individual or
entity to whom they are addressed. If you are not the
intended recipient, please notify admin-mail@alton-
associates.com with "Incorrect Delivery Of Internal
Message" in the subject line along with the exact date
and time you received this message.

All e-mail data may be stored and monitored for the
purposes of security, training and blackmail.

< ATTACHMENT - reviewstat.doc >

Personal Review Statement

In the last year, I feel I have grown both as a person and as an employee. I have taken on the responsibility of a new role with my appointment as Stationery Logistics Manager and feel that I have not only risen to the challenge of this challenging and necessary role, but made it my own through sweeping reforms of the supplies ordering system.

I have been punctual with regard to my time-keeping skills, avoiding tardiness and always arriving at work at or before the correct time. Also, my morale on arriving at work has been good, with far less instances of frustration, inattentiveness and crying. My workstation is always well organised, which reflects my commitment to efficient work practices and not cluttering up the place. Unlike some other employees, I do not misuse company Blu-Tak by affixing photographs of family or loved ones to my cubicle.

I am a valuable member of the team, with important knowledge of many key processes. Without my input, for example, the database of non-standard contracts (H-N) would be virtually unusable, as I'm the only one who knows the spreadsheet shortcut that puts the totals at the bottom of all the columns. Also, nobody else in the office has the direct extension number for Greg in IT, or the registration code you need to install new software on the computer. So, if you think about it, there's actually no way you can fire me. I'm literally indispensable. In the past three months, I am the only person to have restocked the cup holder on the water cooler and I know how everyone takes their coffee and I've hidden all the spiral-bound notebooks. Without me, you'll never find them.

From: admin@weightexchange.co.uk
To: temp-032@alton-associates.co.uk
Subject: Buy Alert

Message:

THE WEIGHT EXCHANGE

Buy Alert!
Unique Reference Code: 2348273-0000003
01/11/07 – 12:30:00
User – lastresort79

      Time for lunch! Eat anything with the
           letter P in its name.

 You have: 14 minutes 30 seconds to complete this sale

 Remember the Golden Rule: Timing is quite important!

Once you have completed this transaction please reply to
this e-mail quoting in the subject header the phrase: "I
have completed this transaction [insert buy alert unique
reference code here]. Thank you The Weight Exchange for
another top market tip. No one does it better."

CAUTION!

WET FLOOR!

(do not trip over this sign)

PLEASE REMOVE YOUR CARD.

PLEASE TAKE YOUR MONEY.

PLEASE DON'T MAKE THIS
HARDER THAN IT HAS TO BE.

PLEASE LEAVE NOW.
I CAN HARDLY BEAR
TO LOOK AT YOU.

FOOOD
Where food really sells

The Amazing Wheat-Free, Germ-Free, Calorie-Free* No-Filling Sandwich

These days, fad diets are widely seen as an important and necessary innovation. Sure, they might not be always the healthiest way to get thin, but they are the easiest to market, so we here at **FOOOD** take them super-seriously. That's why we developed our Amazing Wheat-Free, Germ-Free, Calorie-Free* No-Filling Sandwich. When our blue-sky team first floated the idea past our master chefs, they laughed. Then they handed in their notice. After that, we had trouble with the trade descriptions people, and then those worry-heads at the Food Standards Agency. But eventually (with a little help from our lawyers) people really came round to the idea. And we're sure you will too. So enjoy the world's first filling-free sandwich safe in the knowledge that this is the way the world is heading.

* 245 free calories.

AQUA

When you drink AQUA, you're drinking fourteen million years of natural filtration. Sourced only from only the most enigmatic springs, AQUA flows from the very heart of the Himalayas, the Alps, the Rockies and any number of other mountain ranges. It then journeys heroically through streams, rivers and finally the mighty oceans before being lovingly desalinated, bottled and sold to you. So what you taste when you lift our specially designed ergonomic bottle to your mouth is exactly what nature intended – pure unadulterated water, improved and enhanced by our expert waterologists. Enjoy!

This bottle is for the exclusive use of AQUA water. Do not refill. Failure to observe this warning may result in death, serious illness and the waiving of your statutory rights.

INGREDIENTS: Aqua, Water, Moisturising agent, Hydrogen, Oxygen, Trace amounts of wetness.

CERTIFIED ORGANIC

Lunch Menu

――――◆・◆・◆――――

Hellenic Mussels Braised in Vintage Burgundy

A delicate, piquant, confusing dish, evocative in equal parts of Mediterranean hubris and earthy, unfulfilling intercourse. Not suitable for vegans or recovering alcoholics.

Symmetrical Loins of Highland Quail Served on a Bed of Virgin Spinach and Celeriac Hearts

Our chef's exacting standards for this dish demand that we source only the finest cuts of quail from a small farm high in the Hebridean hills, where the verdant fields of swaying heather lend a unique fragrance to the proprietor's firm and matronly breasts.

Non-Sequential Unmarked Fillets of Manatee Presented Somewhat Obsequiously, as if to Atone for Some Previous Unspecified Misdeed

The subtle flavour of manatee is perfectly complemented by the unmistakable zesty overtones of human faeces in this remarkable and altogether unnecessary dish. The characteristic avuncular aroma is due to the inclusion of nine varieties of unidentifiable cheese at the basting stage. This dish has been variously described as "bellicose", "pancratic" and "fish".

Your Pride

In this unique and challenging dish, our Michelin-listed chef will come to your table and present you with a mobile telephone, whereupon you will be expected to contact, in chronological order, every single person you have ever met and apologise to each of them in turn for your many failings as a human being. This will include, but will not be limited to: your arrogance, your selfishness, your pretension, your tendency to be an inconsiderate lover, your poor personal hygiene and your staggering, chronic insincerity. This will be followed by coffee and a selection of Baltic cheeses.

――――◆・◆・◆――――

CONGRATULATIONS!

You chose the F.O. Triple Bun Mammoth Feast Meal because you know what you like. You could have gone small. You could have decided to hold the onion rings. You could have thought, "I can no longer feel my toes, maybe I should just get some soup." But you didn't, and we applaud you.

You're the kind of guy who looks in the mirror and says, "Now this – this I like. Heart disease, schmart disease! That guy's a quack and I'm gonna get him struck off." You're strong. You looked at the salads and thought, "I'm no Judy Garland fan; I'll have a burger." Good on ya! You're the CEO of you!

At FAT SHACK you're always the CEO of you. So don't just hold the salad – fire it!

SPECIAL OFFER

Gosh™ Calming Moisturising Crème and **Girth**™ For Men now come in a handy 2-for-1 **Happy Couple Skincare Pack**, so you and your partner can experience the joy of synchronised moisturising. If you haven't got a partner, feel free to dispose of the superfluous product in whatever way you see fit before returning to your quiet, lonely existence.

Gosh™

Calming Moisturising Crème

Directions for Use

1. Giggle with friends
2. Take a hot, steamy shower
3. Apply **Gosh**™ Calming Moisturising Crème to your delicate face
4. Smooth it over your supple legs as well
5. Tilt your head to one side and rest it on your knee
6. Look playful
7. And yet thoughtful
8. Go out with friends
9. Jostle for position with them as you walk up the high street laughing
10. Think "this is the best I've felt since I discovered those new tampons!"

Caution. If crème gets in your eyes, flap about ineffectually until your boyfriend returns home and helps you wash it out. If **Gosh**™ Calming Moisturising Crème brings you out in a nasty little rash you might want to try **Gosh**™ Calming Moisturising Crème For Delicate Skin. If that brings you out in a rash you're obviously not beautiful enough to use our products.

Ingredients: Aqua, C12-15, Alkyl Benzoate, Propylene Glycol, Glyceryl, Stearate, Glycerin, Nylon-12, Jackson 5, Birmingham 6, Dimethicone, Panthenol (Pro-Vitamin B5), Acrylates/C10-30, Alkyl Acrylate Crosspolymer, Cetearyl Alcohol, Corn Starch Modified, Zinc PCA, Miami CSI, PEG-100, T-1000, Sodium Hydroxide, Sodium Hydroxymethylglycinate, Potassium Sorbate, Lemon Sorbet, Ronnie Corbett, Anthemis Nobilis.

Girth™ *For Men*
Rough Scrub-off Paste

Directions for Use

1. Do some sport
2. Carelessly wash your hulking body
3. Slap a handful of **Girth**™ Rough Scrub-off Paste onto your freshly shaven man-face
4. Laugh heartily
5. Wipe off any excess paste with a towel
6. A navy blue towel
7. Tilt your head to one side and look into the mirror
8. Run your hand along the rough edge of your shaven skin
9. Allow your wife/girlfriend to put her arms around you from behind
10. Smile contentedly

Caution. If paste gets in your eyes, you may well become the laughing stock of your friends. Grin and bear it. Laugh. If blindness persists, see your doctor; just don't make a big song and dance about it.

Ingredients: Aqua, C12-15, Alkyl Benzoate, Propylene Glycol, Glyceryl, Stearate, Glycerin, Nylon-12, Jackson 5, Birmingham 6, Dimethicone, Panthenol (Pro-Vitamin B5), Acrylates/C10-30, Alkyl Acrylate Crosspolymer, Cetearyl Alcohol, Corn Starch Modified, Zinc PCA, Miami CSI, PEG-100, T-1000, Sodium Hydroxide, Sodium Hydroxymethylglycinate, Potassium Sorbate, Lemon Sorbet, Ronnie Corbett, Anthemis Nobilis, Manliness.

PRODUCT RECALL

Any of our customers who have purchased **GentleCare Moisturising Skin Butter With Soothing Coconut Balm (220ml)** within the last two months are urged to return their purchase as soon as possible for a free replacement product of equal or greater value. Due to an error in the production process, a rogue batch of this product was found to contain jagged pieces of broken glass up to an inch in length.

Additionally, any customer in possession of **Precious Gift Apple And Honey Flavour Baby Food (170ml)** with a Best Before date of March 2010 should return this product immediately, as laboratory tests have shown it to contain traces of nicotine, cyanide and tiny hand-written notes with swear words on.

Finally, all bottles of **Nature's Choice Dairy-Free Calcium Drink (300ml)** should be returned as soon as possible since the company which manufactures them recently announced that their entire dairy-free range did, in fact, contain dairy. In the case of **Nature's Choice Dairy-Free Calcium Drink (300ml)**, the revised list of ingredients is as follows:

INGREDIENTS:
Milk (300ml).

We thank you for your cooperation.

Coca Leaf Powder
(erythroxylon)

For centuries, Coca Leaf Powder has been used as a stimulant for body and mind. It's been known to cure all sorts of ailments such as tiredness, headaches and drunkenness.

Science* has proved that even a small pinch of Coca Leaf Powder can massively boost the brain's activity. Why not try rubbing this soap into your gums after lunch instead of your usual coffee fix?

At Yum! we use pure, genuine Coca Leaf Powder in our products when we want to invigorate you and get you ready for the long day ahead. You'll find it in our Perk-Up Massage Bar, Lovin' It Bath Jellies, ADDIKT Shower Balls, Mental Shampoo or from behind the counter in gram or half-gram bags.

* Our Border Collie

YUM!

There's Great Fun for all the Family at

THE
EMBASSY
HISTORY
MUSEUM!

This Christmas, why not take your nauseating offspring on an action-packed day out at *The Embassy History Museum*? Give in to the niggling worry at the back of your head that says, "If I don't take them to something cultural, they'll grow up as pig-ignorant as me. Or worse, her!" Watch their tiny snot-stained faces light up as they see our bright displays, dumbed down so much that even the most wretched of consumerist whores like you will understand them.

Yes, come to *The Embassy History Museum* and feel embarrassed at the complete lack of anything in your vapid skull every time little Johnny asks you a question about an exhibit.

Monday – Saturday: **10 a.m. – 6 p.m.**
Sunday: **11 a.m. – 4 p.m.**

Entry to the museum is free! However, we do suggest the following donations:

Adults	**£3**
Children	**£15**

Donations are based on how irritating the museum staff find the patrons.

And don't even think about not making a donation, you cheapskate! You gladly pay £10 to go to the cinema and watch the kind of pallid crap that passes for film these days. But can you spare a few quid for the museum? Like fuck you can't! Within these four walls are held the secrets and mysteries of the entire human race. But oh no, it's not a fucking talking robot is it? Or Harry Potter. Harry Potter! You'd think no one had ever written a fucking book before Harry Potter! And you can bet that's where they'd rather go – to see *Harry Potter*! But remember the voice. Yeah! Yeah! The niggling voice! Now look at her! Her! Ahh, that got ya – History Museum it is. But we know your type, you see this as work. Shit work you'd rather not do, and you're not going to pay for that, are you? "Why should I?" you're thinking. "There's no law. I don't HAVE to." So walk past! Just walk past! You, in your Dolce & Gabbana coat! You, in your soft leather brogues with your Blackberry Pearl! You, jiggling the keys to your ridiculous 4x4! All of you safe in the knowledge that "You don't need to know about the Cretaceous period to work in hedge funds, know what I mean." You bastards! You pathetic, bleak, arrogant bastards who won't rest till you've sucked this world dry of anything that brings the rest of us joy. You – with your soirées and your Jamiroquai CDs! You – with your outdoor heaters and gas BBQs. You – who bought *The Da Vinci Code*. How do you sleep at night? You cruel, ignorant, arrogant, insufferable, worthless pieces of shit. I hope you choke on your fucking paninis.

We'll see you soon at *The Embassy History Museum*.
We don't want you here, but it's the only
way we can get our research grant.

PAGETURNERS

Staff Picks

EMPTY GLASS by DR NAÏAN FEDLER

This is a book that changes lives. I first read it four years ago, and I haven't stopped thinking about it. There are so many self-help books out there that it can be hard to know which ones to trust. If you read the wrong one, it could scar you permanently and actually make things a lot worse, but Empty Glass is different. Everything, from the introduction to the ISBN, makes sense in ways you won't even be able to describe. Before I read this book, life seemed pointless and I was ready to end it all, but now things are a lot better. As long as I have this book, everything will be okay. If there's only one copy on the shelf, please don't buy it.

Jenny

EMPTY GLASS
A New Approach to Self-Help

Introduction

Hello. My name is Dr Naïan Fedler. You don't know me yet, but over the next two hundred and thirty-nine pages, you and I will go on a journey together. Along the way, we'll encounter many obstacles. Together, we're going to overcome those obstacles and end our journey exactly where we began, but wiser and with cold air in our lungs.

If this sounds familiar, it's because what I've just described isn't just the way this book works; it's the way life works for each and every one of us. The story I've just outlined is one that you're bound to recognise because it's the very story you're living right now – the story in which you are the main character. Also, I mentioned something similar in the introduction to my last book, *Think Yourself Lucky*, so you might remember it from there.

When you set out on the journey of life, you don't know what to expect. Partly this is because you're very young at the time, but partly it's because life is unpredictable. In fact, I'd go one step further and say that life isn't just unpredictable: it's random. That's a very hard word to fully understand, but it's one that we'll keep coming back to again and again in the course of this book. When you say the word "random", a lot of people think of something like a game of dice or a lottery, but the truth is that the world we live in is far more complicated than we can possibly understand. Imagine a lottery where, instead of choosing numbers, you have to draw a doodle on a piece of paper and if your doodle matches precisely, millimetre for millimetre, the winning one, you get a prize that could be anything from eternal life to instant death. Except that you never get to see the winning doodle, or find out if you've won, until it's far, far too late. And the rules change with every passing second. And no one's quite sure if they're actually playing or not. Or whether the game even exists.

If this sounds daunting, that's because it is. The universe is infinitely complex and you can never hope to understand any part of it, let alone change any aspect of it in any meaningful way. Understanding this is the key to my approach, and the subject of this book's first chapter, *You Are Nothing*.

In order to form a sense of self-worth, you must first recognise that there is not really, in any appreciable sense, such a thing as "self". Far from being an autonomous and self-aware agent of physical action, you are little more than a ragged bundle of chemicals lost in the infinite chaos of an unintelligible universe. Seen from a perspective of unbiased objectivity, you are no more significant than the chair in which you are sitting, the air you breathe or the rotting orange peel you throw in your compost bin. In fact, one day you will become compost right along with that orange peel – your physical body will decay and become indistinguishable from the mulch under your feet. This is the subject of chapter two, *You Are Dying*.

In my professional capacity as a counsellor, a lot of people come to me looking for guidance. Often it's because they feel lost, because they feel scared or because they're worried that they lack direction in life. Over the years, I've thought about these problems and come up with a few answers. In a very simplified form, they go like this:

1. *You are lost.*
2. *You should be scared.*
3. *There is no "direction" you can have other than the slow, inevitable march towards death and, thereafter, oblivion.*

Sometimes, people are resistant to my approach. They say, "Naïan, surely there must be some kind of purpose to life? Or if not a purpose, then at least a way to stay afloat in this vast, bewildering sea of meaninglessness? Or, if nothing else, a way for me to get out of paying for this session?" But to them I say, "You, my friend," (this is merely a turn of phrase – I am fully aware that the people I counsel are clients rather than friends and I would never transgress the boundaries of that professional relationship for both clinical and legal reasons) "are like a clumsy Egyptian boatman." I then leave a gap of precisely two seconds before revealing the punchline:

"You're in denial!" This little joke helps to relieve the tension, but also serves to illustrate a valid psychological point. To deny the fundamental lack of meaning at the heart of all things is to deny a universal truth, and anyone trying to lead their life with that kind of contradiction in the back of their mind is going to end up, like our maladroit African friend, coming a cropper.

Some people try to solve the problem of meaninglessness by relying on the idea of a higher power. For some it's a god or gods, for some it's a commitment to furthering human understanding, for some it's a devotion to altruistic works. Whatever form this delusion takes, my diagnosis is the same. I call these people "head-in-the-sand birds" (the term "ostriches", which I used in my previous books, has since been registered as a trademark by Dr Fenton McWheely, the author of *How Not To Grieve*). By denying the pointlessness of every aspect of existence, these people are setting up a destructive dichotomy, or *destrotomy*, at the centre of their spiritual lives. If they came to me for advice, I would tell them this: it is only by accepting the fundamental emptiness of all things that you can learn to give your life the value it deserves, which is none. We'll discuss this in greater depth in chapter seven, *Nothing To Live For*.

As you read this book, you will come across ideas that challenge you and exercises you may find difficult. My approach to self-help is, I will be the first to admit, radically different from anything that has come before, but this is what makes it so powerful. Whether you've picked up this book as a result of bereavement, unemployment, marital breakdown or simply a lingering sense of dissatisfaction with life, I guarantee that by the time you finish reading it, you'll be seeing things in a whole new way. Next to the dark emptiness of a soulless and chaotic world, your problems will simply fall away into the background. When you and I reach the end of our journey together and turn the last page of chapter thirteen, *Nothing Means Anything, So Fuck It*, I promise you that you'll be a new person: a clear-sighted, rational and, above all, fundamentally empty person.

Thanks for reading.

PAGETURNERS

Staff Picks

FIGHTING FISH IN THE LATE-NIGHT LAUNDROMAT by ZOE FRIEL

A transcendental, bawdy, heartbreaking, disturbing, hilarious, thought-provoking and ubiquitous second novel, this is the book that everyone's talking about. It even has a quote on the cover from the author of the last book that everyone was talking about. A BBC tie-in documentary can't be too far down the pipeline. Now available in hardback, paperback, audiobook and just the empty dust jacket for you to hold in front of your face on public transport.

Anna

FIGHTING FISH IN THE LATE NIGHT LAUNDROMAT

By Zoe Friel

Okay. So. Since you ask, a description of Jim. At least I think he was called Jim. Let's just say for the purposes of this book, he's called Jim. And he's our hero. Jim was six foot, maybe more, maybe less, blondey/browny/mousy hair, big nose, earring. He might have had a tattoo. He laughed in a way that suggested he'd been abused as a child. He spoke French, poorly. He spoke Spanish with a Cockney accent. He loved the idea of China. He dreamed of doing the London Marathon.

Is that enough? Have you got a mental picture yet? It doesn't really matter. Jim might have existed, he might not have. It doesn't matter. What matters is the story. What matters is that you're listening. What matters is that we can tell stories, and through stories we change. This is a story about change. And yes, it does feature Jim. And yes, he is real. At least, he was to me.

Throw your frazzled brains back to a time when Prince was still Prince and no one really thought of him as an artist anyway. A time before blue Smarties. A time when to be blue wasn't smart. A time when *Smash Hits* was 'in touch'. A time . . .

It was a Friday. Or Thursday. It doesn't matter. What does matter is that it was a school day and school days were not like weekends. That was, if you went to school. And we did. We all did. In a way, we all still do. But in another way, not.

It was third lesson. The lesson after break. Teenage minds humming with the true lessons of life, the one you learnt out of class. The lessons that weren't on the national curriculum, lessons that you'd keep on learning for the rest of your life. That's what I meant when I said we were still all at school, in some ways. Unless I meant something else. Which I did.

1

PAGETURNERS

Staff Picks

THE FIREGARDENS OF AKHLAHAD
by STUART ISINGLEY

This is the third book of the excellent Darkened Things Revealed series by Stuart Isingley. It will appeal to both fans of the genre and newcomers, although many of the events, characters, places and words will be completely unintelligible without having read the previous two (and subsequent nine) books in the series. Isingley is renowned for his skilled and ornate use of language, as well as for the intimidating length (not to say weight) of his books, even in paperback format.

The Firegardens Of Akhlahad

by Stuart Isingley

BOOK I: ICE OF AGES

– Chapter One –

It was a night like any other in the secret city of Reaha'tung, hidden from the glowering red skies of the endless winter by an ornate, imposing wall of rough-hewn grey stones brought from the quarries of Ksorah, far to the north, or, as the cityfolk of Reaha'tung called it, The Cold North. Mist swirled round the ornate cast-iron poles that lined the streets, each holding aloft a single glowing ball of Wyr'kara in order to light the cobbled paths of the city for its night-dwelling inhabitants, their hands thrust deep into the pockets of their ornate, tightly fastened coats as they hurried through the dark velvet night on their many errands, be they innocent or, as in the case of Elhirir the Thief, not so innocent.

He scythed through the mist like the sharp, curved blade of the ornate agricultural tool known by the farmers of the Myalnder Plains as a 'thyske' might slice through towering, ripe corn on a summer's afternoon, when the armies of G'tath call on the humble landworkers for supplies to fuel their seemingly never-ending war with the thronging hordes of the Caedin who first arrived from the east (or, as the farmers of the Myalnder Plains called it, The Mysterious East) so long ago in their dark, mysterious, ornate

1

warships, the prows anointed with the blood of their enemies. Elhirir had business in the ancient temple, the dark forgotten part of this labyrinthine city, where the maze-like paths and alleyways conspired to tangle and knot and deny any visitor (though what visitors the ancient temple could possibly have was a matter known only to those visitors, and since they were not the type of people to talk lightly of such matters, it was hardly information that could be easily gleaned from, say, the chattering crowds of the Reaha'tung market, which took place every two cycles of Hto, the greater of the two moons that sailed through the sky far above the city and its many and various inhabitants, be they Dsala, Khe, Fleebling or Dwarf, for many races lived in the winding streets of this ancient and confusing city, each with their own customs and rituals, not to mention their own food, the mingled smells of which rose daily from the ornate chimneys of a thousand homes) safe egress to their destination, whatever that destination might be. If he was late, it would mean his immediate death. Suddenly, unexpectedly, taking him by surprise, a spectral figure emerged, wraith-like, from the ghostly shadows in front of him.

'Hail,' said the figure.

'Hail,' replied Elhirir, sliding his ornately crafted Sath'tan blade, its edge darkened by the ashes from a ceremonial fire lit in deference to Yethelehe, goddess of assassins and patron of the house of Xvicih, whose armies once, many cycles of Oth ago, marched on the cursed (yet ornate) city of Khraikh and slaughtered all therein, into his hand. 'What business have you with me this night, whosoever you might be?'

'I bear a message,' replied the as-yet-unidentified figure, his face obscured by the darkness of the night and the turgid, clinging fog that hung in front of his shadowy visage, whether by nature or by sorcery it was impossible to say, though there was a strange metallic glint to the edges of the nebulous haze that belied the hand of one of the city's many journeymen of magyk in its creation, 'from one who takes an interest in your affairs.'

2

'And who might that be?' demanded Elhirir, defiantly. 'I care not for those who care not to reveal their identities to those whose cares they care to have a care in.'

'It matters not,' exclaimed the figure.

'It matters not not,' contradicted Elhihir.

'Have a care,' warned the figure, whose voice was hollow and booming, 'for you walk on shifting ground, Elhihir, son of Elhifir. It is as the prophesies have foretold: "When the sky in the north is ablood with the flames of betrayal, the unknown circle of those who are lost must be taken to a place unseen by the anointed few; only then will the long-awaited kin of the moons return to the place from whence arose the rage of he who once sat on the blood-throne of fallen men and held in his hand the ornate sceptre of the lost isles of those whose voices are unheard, their cries unheeded, their prayers unanswered, until the coming of he who wields the power of the heir of all that the sun touches whence it rises unbidden from the valley of the children of the ending of the day of the birth of the people of the sky of the easternmost land, which is now lost but which may be looked upon again, when the path of the mountains of the dawn of the heir of the line of the king of the land of the many who speak in cries of despair is opened once more."'

Elhihir gasped, for these were the exact words he had borne since birth in a tattoo on his left shoulder.

Perki.®

Fanatical brothers Alex and Alexander Hajduk set up their now legendary coffee roastery in the unique surroundings of the Peabody Industrial Estate in Chigwell in 2004, supplying local caterers with an exciting, revolutionary, brilliant coffee bean, fast-roasted in the traditional Polish way. In 2005, their efficient production methods and ability to undercut their Italian rivals meant they had amassed enough hard capital to move into their own premises. Perki opened on Chigwell high street on 7 July 2005 and, despite a tough first day's trading, the company hasn't looked back. There are now 25,000 Perkis all over the UK.

Our Beans
In their raw form, coffee beans are bland, odourless, indigestible and, in the case of our special Polish beans, highly toxic. It's the baking process that brings out the distinctive Perki taste. All our master blenders have the Perki 'Seal of Approval' badge, which requires a three-day course at our headquarters in Milton Keynes.

Our master blenders don't waste valuable time and money sourcing coffee beans from all over the world. Instead, we are the sole purchaser of the NIEBEZPIECZNIE bean grown in our huge organic warehouses near Krakow. Before baking, our blenders mix up the big beans with smaller beans to create the impression of blending.

Our Roasting Process
Our patented 'flash baking' process means that we can bake our beans much faster than other coffee companies roast theirs. It's this that gives our coffee its distinctive 'burnt' flavour. It frustrates us to see these fledgling companies slow-roasting their beans. It just increases their overheads; it's no wonder we're able to undercut them and take their trading premises off them at a snip.

Locking in the Flavour
As soon as our beans have been baked, we freeze-dry them to lock in the flavour before shipping them to our warehouses. Here, they can be left for up to twelve months to mature before being transported to our coffee houses where they are ground, creating that strong smell you've recently come to associate with coffee.

Perki.® Products.

Perki Slurps	SMALL	MEDIUM	LARGE	SILLY
Café Latte The Milky One	£1.50	£1.75	£2.00	£2.01
Cappuccino The Frothy One	£1.50	£1.75	£2.00	£2.01
Mocha The Chocolatey One	£1.60	£1.85	£2.10	£2.11
Espresso The one when you don't get very much but you don't want very much anyway	£1.50	XXX	XXX	£1.51
Machiatta The Made-up One	£1.70	XXX	XXX	£1.71
Filter Coffee It's Filter Coffee	£1.20	£1.35	£1.60	£1.61

Skinny Blueberry Muffin

Exercise Price: Quick jog around the park

Full-Fat Blueberry Muffin

Exercise Price: 15 mins bike / 10 mins treadmill / full cardio workout

Double Choc-Chip Muffin

Exercise Price: Basically we're talking a week of intensive workouts here. That means getting up at 6 a.m. to get to the gym before work because you know you're going to be too knackered to do it after you've been behind that desk for eight hours. Is it worth it? Really? I mean, is it?

Double Choc-Chip-Fudge-Caramel Surprise Muffin

Exercise Price: You do realise that this is it, don't you? You eat this and you'll never fit into that pair of skinny jeans again. Sure, one muffin can't make you fat for ever, but once you make a decision to buy something like this you've crossed a personal line it's impossible to come back from. You're of a certain age now; you can't just put it on, knock it off, put it on, knock it off like you used to. This is it. Decision time. But far be it from me, a humble price tag, to tell you what to do with your life. I will say this, though: when you're buying two airline seats for every journey and Channel 4 are knocking at your door wanting to make a sympathetic documentary with a headline-grabbing title, don't come crying to me because I will simply say I told you so. I'm a price tag and I deal in harsh realities.

WARNING!

These doors open and close automatically. Please try not to get involved in a hilarious slapstick routine with them. It won't be as funny as you think it is and the laughter of your co-workers will be born of pity, not the joy of a shared experience.

From: hrm@alton-associates.co.uk
To: group@alton-associates.co.uk
Subject: Today's Second Key Thought

Message:

Don't be afraid to go the extra mile for your customer
- there is always a slightly more expensive product
to push them towards. And if there isn't, charge them
double for the existing one.

Alton Associates: Understanding the service/profit
dynamic.

This e-mail and any files transmitted with it are private
and intended solely for the use of the individual or
entity to whom they are addressed. If you are not the
intended recipient, please notify admin-mail@alton-
associates.co.uk with "Incorrect Delivery Of Internal
Message" in the subject line along with the exact date
and time you received this message.

All e-mail data may be stored and monitored for the
purposes of security, training and blackmail.

From: admin@weightexchange.co.uk
To: temp-032@alton-associates.co.uk
Subject: Buy Alert

Message:

THE WEIGHT EXCHANGE

Buy Alert!
Unique Reference Code: 2348273-0000004
01/11/07 - 12:44:03
User - lastresort79

                    Eat a warm pasta salad.

            You have: 04 minutes 00 seconds
                 to complete this sale

              Remember the Golden Rule:
              Timing is quite important!

Once you have completed this transaction please reply to
this e-mail quoting in the subject header the phrase: "I
have completed this transaction [insert buy alert unique
reference code here]. Thank you The Weight Exchange for
another top market tip. No one does it better."

From: admin@weightexchange.co.uk
To: temp-032@alton-associates.co.uk
Subject: Buy Alert REMINDER!

Message:

THE WEIGHT EXCHANGE

Buy Alert! REMINDER!
Unique Reference Code: 2348273-0000005
01/11/07 - 12:47:53
User - lastresort79

        Eat a warm pasta salad NOW!

      You have: 00 minutes 10 seconds
         to complete this sale

        Remember the Golden Rule:
       Timing is quite important!

Once you have completed this transaction please reply to
this e-mail quoting in the subject header the phrase: "I
have completed this transaction [insert buy alert unique
reference code here]. Thank you The Weight Exchange for
another top market tip. No one does it better."

From: admin@weightexchange.co.uk
To: temp-032@alton-associates.co.uk
Subject: Buy Alert EMERGENCY!

Message:

THE WEIGHT EXCHANGE

EMERGENCY!
Unique Reference Code: 2348273-0000006
01/11/07 - 12:51:03
User - lastresort79

MARKET CRASH!
MARKET CRASH!
MARKET CRASH!

Take emergency sell strip NOW to rebalance market! You
have been transferred to instant
text alerts for your safety! Await further instructions!

You have: 00 minutes 00 seconds
to complete this sale

Remember the Golden Rule:
Timing is quite important!

Once you have completed this transaction please reply to
this e-mail quoting in the subject header the phrase: "I
have completed this transaction [insert buy alert unique
reference code here]. Thank you The Weight Exchange for
another top market tip. No one does it better."

From: officework
To: temp-032@alton-associates.co.uk
Subject: NOW IS THE SPECIAL TIME!

Message:

So with stock market and RICHES of $$$ the dollar
INVESTMENT OPPORTUNITY!

With Amazing and the TAX FREE OPPORTUNITY of moneys with
exchange Rating of BENEFIT INSTANTS because always the
systems because

BUY SELL HIGH LOW!

GUARANTEE! fear dies being OPPORTUNITY for $$$ and STOCK
MARKET with GOLD bring you and life becoming EASY now
LACK OF WORRY opportunity No

SLEEPLESS NIGHT because GENUINE $$$ work hard and
SECURITY of alway's KNOWLEDGE beyond living and Now

light which BREAKS on far away HORIZON! RESTLESS sleep
of LIVING and Worldly Concern become AS NOTHING! So now
is it ALL.

DEATH ending as ZERO PROBLEM with guarantee $$$ and
ENDLESS JOYS before dark forgetting ! become CREATED at
HAPPINESS with
neverending before night
and night and
night.

From: j.kemp@alton-associates.co.uk
To: salesgroup2@alton-associates.co.uk
Subject: Magimix

Message:

My Magimix has been left in a filthy state and in bits
all across the kitchen surface. This was a Christmas
present from my husband so I could make my soups at
work.

Personal belongings are the most valuable and special
things in life and we should all respect each other's
right NOT to have to share.

Jenny

This e-mail and any files transmitted with it are private
and intended solely for the use of the individual or
entity to whom they are addressed. If you are not the
intended recipient, please notify admin-mail@alton-
associates.co.uk with "Incorrect Delivery Of Internal
Message" in the subject line along with the exact date
and time you received this message.

All e-mail data may be stored and monitored for the
purposes of security, training and blackmail.

From: dave_boy@ezmail.com
To: temp-032@alton-associates.co.uk
Subject: Fwd: I laughed till I shat!

Message:

Hey guys. I don't normally do this, but I had to let you
see these. Brightened up my day!

D

A guy goes into a brothel and finds the girl he wants. He
takes her upstairs and the next thing everyone outside
can hear her shouting, "No, no! Don't do it that way!"
The Madam goes to the room and asks what the problem is.
"He says he wants to do it the way he does back home,"
the girl says. "So let him," says the Madam. Ten minutes
later, the man leaves. "What was the problem?" the Madam
asks. "Well," says the girl, "he said that back home, he
gets to do it for free!"

Two guys are sitting in a bar. One turns to the other
and says, "Hey, do you like big asses on women?" "Hell
no," his friend says. "Well do you like droopy breasts?"
"No way," his friend replies. "What about loose sloppy
c**ts?" he asks. "No!" says his friend. "Well," the guy
says, "if you don't like fat asses and droopy breasts
and loose sloppy c**ts, why are you sneaking round with
my wife when I'm at work?"

A guy asks his buddy, "Hey, what happened to that girl
you had?" "She got syphilis and bled to death," his buddy
replies. "You don't bleed to death with syphilis," he
says. His buddy winks at him. "You do if you give it to me!"

A newly married couple are in bed on their wedding night.
"Well darling," says the young wife, "this is it. You
can do whatever you want to me." So he beats her to
death, takes all her money and gets a hooker. He f**ks
the hooker in a pool of his dead wife's blood, then kills
her as well and defecates on the corpse. When the police
finally arrive, they find him lying naked in the bath with
a shotgun in his hand and half his face missing. Several
of the police officers on the scene later show signs of
deep-seated psychological trauma as a result of the
experience. These post-traumatic symptoms lead, in at
least one case, to long-term depression, alcoholism and,
three years later, a divorce in which custody of the
children is given to the grandparents.

WELCOME TO WEIGHT
EXCHANGE TEXT
ALERTS. You have
been placed on
this list due to
mismanagement
and/or insider
trading. Drink a
glass of water.
You have 01m 12s.

From: dconnolly@alton-associates.co.uk
To: ac31-team4-group@alton-associates.co.uk
Subject: Re: Knees Up!

Message:

Guys!

I haven't had a single e-mail back off you yet. Come on
people. Am I the only one who likes getting so smashed
out of his brain he can't even order his kebab? – "I'll
have a dixed monger, pleesse." – remember that CLASSIC,
Dukesy?!!

The Daz Man

This e-mail and any files transmitted with it are private
and intended solely for the use of the individual or
entity to whom they are addressed. If you are not the
intended recipient, please notify admin-mail@alton-
associates.co.uk with "Incorrect Delivery Of Internal
Message" in the subject line along with the exact date
and time you received this message.

All e-mail data may be stored and monitored for the
purposes of security, training and blackmail.

Search Results

Great prices on **BORED** today!
…click now click now click now for GREAT PRICES and AMAZING
PRICES on all your **BORED** needs…
www.genericshop.com/user_response.stm

Things to do when you're **bored**
…so if I'm **bored** I just phone up a friend, turn on the TV or pray
for salvation from Jesus, who died…
www.never**bored**withgod.com/index.html

Tales from the Quarry
…next step was to deploy the NK88, which **bored** a hole roughly
the size of a human head. Once it had **bored**…
www.miningforfunandprofit.org/quarrytales.htm

The **Bored** have officially split
…and it just seemed like everything we did had been done before,
like there's only twelve notes, you know? And it turned out there
was actually already a band called "**Bored**", so we thought…
www.backroombandnetwork.com/user/the**bored**

True Mining Stories
…next step was to deploy the NK88, which **bored** a hole roughly
the size of a human head. Once it had **bored**…
www.trueminingstories.com/quarry.htm

Bored With Being Misunderstood?
…Handy Guide To Web Slang When the Internet was first invented,
it was intended for use as an academic…
www.slangexplainedforyou.com/node/8345/
boredandmisunderstood/1.html

A Handy Guide To Web Slang

When the Internet was first invented, it was intended for use as an academic repository of essays, research papers, scholarly works and pornography. Now, almost a decade later, there are hundreds, if not thousands, of "web" pages, providing everything from national train timetables to local bus timetables. There are even pages where ordinary people, without a specialised knowledge of computers, can talk to each other by using the "keyboard" as if it were a typewriter. Of course, the Internet only has a limited amount of space, so conversations are often conducted in a kind of shorthand. This slang (known to aficionados as "slang") can often seem bewildering, complicated and upsetting to someone more used to doing their talking in "RL" (Real Life). Luckily, we've compiled a list of commonly used phrases, so you never have to fear the "web speak" of teenagers again.

FYI = For Your Information

LOL = Laughing Out Loud

ROTFLOL = Rolling On The Floor Laughing Out Loud

SCI = Secretly Crying Inside

IMO = In My Opinion

IMHO = In My Humble Opinion

IMNSHO = In My Not So Humble Opinion

IMRIIO = In My Ridiculous, Ill-Informed Opinion

OMG = Oh My God!

BTTOG = By The Trunk Of Ganesh!

ISOTBOMA = I Swear On The Bones Of My Ancestors

IIWSFOCTLAIMAHSTS = If I Wasn't So Focused On Constructing This Lengthy Acronym, I Might Actually Have Something To Say

TSIC = This Soup Is Cold

PTIAABMANO = Please Take It Away And Bring Me A New One

WDYMYHGAMITSOTD = What Do You Mean You Haven't Got Any More? It's The Soup Of The Day

VWCYPJHTOUFM = Very Well. Could You Please Just Heat This One Up For Me?

TIR = This Is Ridiculous

IDTTTYM = I Demand To Talk To Your Manager

WWWHBB = Well, When Will He Be Back?

FIWH = Fine, I'll Wait Here

CIHACOCP = Could I Have A Cup Of Coffee Please?

OS = One Sugar

TY = Thank You

WEIGHT EXCHANGE:
Drink banana-
flavoured milk
through a novelty
straw. You have
54m 01s.

Search Results

Great prices on **NOVELTY STRAW** today!
...click now click now click now for GREAT PRICES and AMAZING
PRICES on all your **NOVELTY STRAW** needs...
www.genericshop.com/user_response.stm

You could be drinking everything through a **novelty straw**
...find that drinks just fly by when you're slurping through a **straw**
shaped like a pair of glasses, a snake, or a semi-detached house...
www.**novelty**jokeshop.com

Novelty Items Top **Straw** Poll
...found that the most popular intra-office birthday gifts were
novelty items such as whoopee cushions, fake breasts and
inflatable genitalia. Instances of workplace depression...
www.superteamsynergy.com/moraleboost/pollresults.html

Novelty Wears Off For **Straw**
...a separate development, **Straw** commented that he was "sick
and tired of people eulogising this wretched girl", a comment
which caused...
www.new-newest-news.co.uk/article/130906/**straw**.html

Judge Rules **Novelty Straw** Manufacturer Responsible For Family Death
...what he called a "grave error of misjudgement", Judge David Ely
condemned the policy and practices of "Fun Fun...
www.new-newest-news.co.uk/article/100906/**straw**death.html

Novelty Holidays – The Magic of **Straw**henge
...years ago, the druids of Bellingthorpe Metropolitan District built
a structure that would have been visible from space...
www.**novelty**holidays.com/visitengland/**straw**henge.htm

Visit Strawhenge!

Four thousand years ago, the druids of the Bellingthorpe Metropolitan District built a structure that would have been visible from space. Space flight was not to be perfected for another 3,950 years, but their efforts were not in vain.

To this very day, the site on which Strawhenge once stood is an awe-inspiring and sacred place. At the confluence of what National Trust guidelines prevent us from describing as four ley lines, Strawhenge is a focal point for huge amounts of alleged spiritual energy. In fact, if you stand motionless on a clear night and listen very carefully, the druids who once walked this land can still be heard echoing across the ages (again, National Trust guidelines require us to clarify that this is not literally true).

Of course, the original straw from which the henge was constructed has long since fallen and been taken into the earth from whence it came (rotted), but we have lovingly recreated the layout of this unique historical site by placing concrete markers at the locations of the original structures. By consulting our colour-coded map, you can (just about) visualise the mighty henge in all its original glory.

Strawhenge is a fantastic day out for all the family, a slice of living history for school trips and a real treat for anyone who likes looking at nondescript concrete bollards in the middle of a wet field.

Search Results

Great prices on **RELIGIOUS EXPERIENCE** today!
...click now click now click now for GREAT PRICES and AMAZING
PRICES on all your **RELIGIOUS EXPERIENCE** needs...
www.genericshop.com/user_response.stm

RELIGIOUS EXPERIENCE
...and see the world's first and only theme park based entirely on
the Truth of Scripture. Ride the Exodus Coaster out of Egyptland!
Get soaked on the Baby Moses Log Flume! Play Snakes and
Apples in the Edendome and...
www.**religiousexperience**parkohio.com

Blow Your Mind: The Truth
...because in my **experience**, people who describe themselves as
religious or whatever are just conforming to this whole mind-killing
numbness about just swallowing whatever **religious**...
www.blowyourmind.net/opinion/jaxxon/index.html

Religious Experience – BlogPedia
...many instances of so-called **religious experiences** which, when
subjected to exacting scrutiny, fail to live up to the hyperbolic...
www.blogpedia.org/**religious_experience**

Reviewthereviews.com: Avatar
...and far from being a **"religious experience"**, the live show was
the kind of mess of feedback and lazy performance that you might
expect from...
www.reviewthereviews.com/thread/h342e-75/avatar.html

: : : avatar : : :
...of what critics have described as a **"religious experience"** in
musical form. As well as universal critical acclaim, their debut
album has been played to hospice patients suffering from terminal
cancer, who instantly...
www.avatartheband.com

AVATAR

NEWS/GIGS/RELEASES/INFO/CONTACT

Dark clouds hang low over a crouching world. Endless shadowed cities stretch out as far as the eye can see, streetlights burning like funeral pyres. Each building stands like a dim silhouetted tombstone against the turbulent sky. A cold, dry wind snakes through the empty streets, carrying with it the detritus of a thousand forgotten lives. This is a nowhere time, a nowhere place. But then…

Like a shaft of sunlight breaking through the clouds, like the sudden coming of spring to an endless winter, like the first blast of the clarion call to salvation, it begins: **avatar**. Like a spinning cube of pure energy deep in the heart of a dying star, **avatar** are not so much a band as a phenomenon; not so much a phenomenon as an epiphany; not so much an epiphany as a transcendental victory of marketing over reality. At once a wave, a particle and a five-piece rock outfit, **avatar** defy the gravity of musical convention and create a truly unique, heart-stopping, genre-less über-aesthetic, reminiscent in equal parts of a profound religious experience and listening to Oasis on a mobile phone.

Through a subtle blend of three-chord pub rock, back-combed hair and ambient guerrilla marketing, **avatar** have quickly become the most important band on the contemporary British music scene. With appearances on national television and radio, as well as interviews in broadsheet newspapers and over-excited articles in the music press, there can hardly be a person left in North London who doesn't jut their chin upwards at their name in a gesture of vague recognition.

avatar are as ubiquitous as they are ambitious, with their latest EP becoming the first ever record to top the charts purely on the basis of ringtone sales. Hailed as the "Record of the Millennium" by the NME, their forthcoming live album features no less than seven ironic cover versions of eighties pop classics. Their meteoric rise to stardom will be matched only by their stalwart resistance in the face of the next big thing, expected to be some kind of avant-garde bluegrass disco pop.

Unexpected Error (-304)

Due to you selecting an option that probably
seemed perfectly reasonable at the time, this
application has performed an illegal operation
and will be shut down. I can't help but notice
that it's been about half an hour since you
saved, so you're probably feeling a certain
amount of frustration about now.

Click the link below to send an error report.
[ERRORTYPE:ENNUI]

HEY. THOUGHT YOU MIGHT LIKE TO SIGN THIS. IT'S FOR WHATSHERFACE — GIRL WITH SPECS WHO SITS NEAR CLARKY. YOU KNOW.

14:50

ALL THE BEST AND GOOD LUCK IN YOUR NEW JOB!

You'll be missed!

Pop back and see us whenever you can! Good luck!

ENJOY YOUR NEW JOB YOU LUCKY GIT! ONLY JOKING! (NOT JOKING!!!)

I'M SURE YOU'LL HAVE A GREAT TIME AT LITTLETONS — THEY'RE ALL MAD THERE (JUST LIKE YOU!) NO PANDA IMPRESSIONS, THOUGH, IF YOU REMEMBER THAT. YOU DON'T WANT THEM THINKING YOU'RE AN OFFICE "BAMBOO" (BIMBO)! THAT'D BE "PANDERING" (PANDA-ING) TO THEM MORE THAN THEY COULD "BEAR" (PANDA BEAR).

I've always loved you. It was me that kept leaving you those silent answer phone messages. It wasn't meant to be scary, I just never got the courage to say anything. I'm sorry. I always imagined we'd one day get married and have kids. I guess I missed my chance. Go! Just go! And remember whatever happens you can die knowing that someone loved you once.

SEE YA.

Who wrote that? It's creepy. Good luck! xx

It was Dave. He was only taking the piss. Yeah, all the best.

I don't think we ever spoke. But good luck with it all anyway.

Great news about the new job. Well done. You're still welcome to come on the team night out on the 16th. Should be a lot of fun. Please come. Bring some people from your new work. Or friends. Or relatives.

From: hrm@alton-associates.co.uk
To: group@alton-associates.co.uk
Subject: Today's Final Key Thought

Message:

Think of your team as a family – a family you get paid
to spend time with.

Alton Associates: There's no "I" in synergy.

This e-mail and any files transmitted with it are private
and intended solely for the use of the individual or
entity to whom they are addressed. If you are not the
intended recipient, please notify admin-mail@alton-
associates.co.uk with "Incorrect Delivery Of Internal
Message" in the subject line along with the exact date
and time you received this message.

All e-mail data may be stored and monitored for the
purposes of security, training and blackmail.

From: dconnolly@alton-associates.co.uk
To: ac31-team4-group@alton-associates.co.uk
Subject: Re: Knees Up!

Message:

Dear Blue Team,

Unfortunately it seems like quite a few members can't make it on Friday. Dan and Suz are both going away for the weekend – they assure me it's separately, but you never know. Nudge nudge, wink wink! ;-) And it seems that pretty much everyone else is going to Pete and Sheila's wedding on Saturday and so they want to get an early night.

Looks like we might have to postpone the 'Team Piss Up' (as it's lovingly known) until the new year, as it also seems you guys are mostly booked until Christmas. Me and Luce will still be larging it up (her fiance Dave will be there too). We're going to be at The Camel after work, from about 6 p.m. (1800 hours – yeah, yeah, I know, Steve. Ever heard of a typo, mate?). If any of you want to join us at any point in the evening, please do. Bring your mates and/or family along. It'll be a laugh, whatever.

All the best, guys,

Darren

This e-mail and any files transmitted with it are private and intended solely for the use of the individual or entity to whom they are addressed. If you are not the intended recipient, please notify admin-mail@alton-associates.co.uk with "Incorrect Delivery Of Internal Message" in the subject line along with the exact date and time you received this message.

All e-mail data may be stored and monitored for the purposes of security, training and blackmail.

From: j.kemp@alton-associates.co.uk
To: salesgroup2@alton-associates.co.uk
Subject: Dance Mat

Message:

Somebody has used my dance mat and now it's all scuffed.
I would like reimbursing.

Jenny

This e-mail and any files transmitted with it are private
and intended solely for the use of the individual or
entity to whom they are addressed. If you are not the
intended recipient, please notify admin-mail@alton-
associates.co.uk with "Incorrect Delivery Of Internal
Message" in the subject line along with the exact date
and time you received this message.

All e-mail data may be stored and monitored for the
purposes of security, training and blackmail.

WEIGHT EXCHANGE:
Eat 300kg of raw
turkey mince. You
have 00m 15s.

From: s.ackland@alton-associates.co.uk
To: altonUK@alton-associates.co.uk
Subject: Stapler

Message:

Hi!

Does anyone have a stapler I could use? I've got six or
seven things to staple this afternoon.

All best,

Sandra

This e-mail and any files transmitted with it are private
and intended solely for the use of the individual or
entity to whom they are addressed. If you are not the
intended recipient, please notify admin-mail@alton-
associates.co.uk with "Incorrect Delivery Of Internal
Message" in the subject line along with the exact date
and time you received this message.

All e-mail data may be stored and monitored for the
purposes of security, training and blackmail.

From: admin@weightexchange.co.uk
To: temp-032@alton-associates.co.uk
Subject: Account Cancellation

Message:

THE WEIGHT EXCHANGE

ACCOUNT CANCELLATION
Unique Reference Code: 2348273-XXXXXXX
01/11/07 - 15:38:10
User - lastresort79

At your request, your account with The Weight Exchange
has been terminated. You will still be charged for one
year's membership and will be expected to settle your
account balance in the form of excess body fat.

Thank you for using The Weight Exchange. All
correspondence is now closed. Don't come crying to us
when you're clinically obese, frantically searching
for your shrivelled genitalia under endless folds
of blubber, desperate not to soil yourself for the
thousandth time because you can't - literally can't
- get up to change the bed sheets.

Search Results

Great prices on **ALTERNATIVE DIET** today!
…click now click now click now for GREAT PRICES and AMAZING
PRICES on all your **ALTERNATIVE DIET** needs…
www.genericshop.com/user_response.stm

Looking for an **alternative** to **diet**ing?
…why not try getting really fat? You'll soon find that the body
becomes "self-regulating", with regular bouts of vomiting and…
www.takebackyourbody.org

ItsYourLifestyle.net: Being **Alternative**
…be quite easy to achieve, as long as you know the basic rules.
In order to stand out from the herd and be an individual, you must
observe certain guidelines on clothes, **diet**, attitude…
www.itsyourlifestyle.net/alt.htm

Alternative therapy: For happiness, peace and dieting
…Do you suffer from persistent worry, panic attacks or moments
of doubt?…
www.hypnotherapyworks.org

hypnotherapyworks.org

Do you suffer from persistent worry, panic attacks or moments of doubt? Do you find it difficult to get out of bed in the morning? Have you ever buttered a slice of toast only to let it go cold and throw it away, just because you can't be bothered to find the jam? What you need is **HYPNOTHERAPY**.

The word **HYPNOTHERAPY** literally means therapy through hypnosis, the process of hypnotising someone in order to give them therapy, or "therapeute" them hypnotically. Since its invention by Anton Mesmer, from whose name we get the word "mesmer", literally hundreds of people have benefited from the therapeutic power of hypnotic therapy, or "**HYPNOTHERAPY**". But enough science! How can you make **HYPNOTHERAPY** work for you?

HYPNOTHERAPY can help you to stop smoking, especially if you smoke. It can also be used to cure phobias, such as claustrophobia, homophobia, vertigo or shingles. Let's say you suffer from Arachnophobia™. Through the power of **HYPNOTHERAPY**, you can confront and defeat your fear* and never have to worry again about the quiet scuttling of a million spindly legs in the dead of night, getting closer, ever closer to your vulnerable, sleeping mouth.

When you think of hypnotism, you might think of people eating raw onions, or taking their clothes off and barking like dogs, but those things are very rarely part of genuine **HYPNOTHERAPY**. Instead, **HYPNOTHERAPY** gives you the chance to make a change for the better – to banish your fears, control your urges and become master (or mistress) of your own thoughts. It can even help with emotional turmoil, such as dealing with bereavement. Whether you're mourning the loss of a parent, a partner or a medical licence, **HYPNOTHERAPY** could be the answer, so get in touch today, quoting "WEBSITE-SCAM" for a 12% discount on your first session.

WARNING! Not suitable for those with a history of severe mental illness and/or killing sprees.

* You will not confront or defeat actual spiders.

From: s.ackland@alton-associates.co.uk
To: altonUK@alton-associates.co.uk
Subject: Stapler

Message:

Hi again,

Checked 2nd floor stationery cupboard (thanks for
the tip-off Steve!) but alas, no stapler. Any other
suggestions?

All best,

Sandra

This e-mail and any files transmitted with it are private
and intended solely for the use of the individual or
entity to whom they are addressed. If you are not the
intended recipient, please notify admin-mail@alton-
associates.co.uk with "Incorrect Delivery Of Internal
Message" in the subject line along with the exact date
and time you received this message.

All e-mail data may be stored and monitored for the
purposes of security, training and blackmail.

MeetMeet

The Social Networking site for people who like to MeetMeet

MY PROFILE   MEETMEET TOP 100   SEARCH   EVENT LISTING   SIGN-OUT

Hiya! Welcome to MeetMeet – the social networking site for people who like to MeetMeet. Imagine never losing touch with anyone. Well, with MeetMeet that dream is a reality. Whether it was a bit of uncomfortable eye contact on the tube, or an uncle who made you sit on his knee right up to the age of seventeen, MeetMeet can help you to stay in touch forever.

Not only that! You can use MeetMeet to MeetMeet new friends, to make important contacts for that creative outlet you really should have by now and to groom prospective lovers.

Start building your profile today. Try to think of your profile as an advert – a billboard with your face on it, surrounded by millions of other billboards with other faces on them. Remember, life IS a popularity contest.

Why Not Check Out These Cool MeetMeet Profiles?

Rupert Halfpenny – OUTRAGEOUS comedian and television presenter Rupert Halfpenny is just the sort of chap we like here on MeetMeet. He's über-sexy and a shameless self-promoter. Check out his profile for a video of him doing a hilarious new routine that uses his famous catchphrase – "I'm a plonker for doing them drugs, ain't I?" – an unprecedented 17 times.

Maurice Vanns – After being bombarded with requests from the staff and readers of *Avant-Folk Magazine*, we decided to feature old-timer Maurice Vanns on our front page. Currently making big waves on the Cambridge folk scene, Maurice is the veteran of 9 studio albums, including *The Naked Presidents (Vol. 1)*, out this month on Vannity.

Evangeline Sheppy – Six months ago, no one had heard of 15-year-old Evangeline Sheppy. The music industry dismissed her work as "childish – tuneless, half finished, and with meaningless lyrics". But the hordes of teenage MeetMeet users disagreed, and with over 12 million downloads the record industry is finally taking notice. Check out her new download-only single 'SATs Are Well Shit', from her forthcoming album *Half-Price Travelcard*.

www.meetmeet.co.uk/mauricevanns

maurice vanns

"Folking Heck! It's Maurice Vanns!"

Member since: 14/06/06
Date Today 01/11/07
Last login: 01/11/07

Profile Views: 452

Profile

Maurice Vanns is perhaps best known as one of the most exciting experimental avant-folk troubadours ever to come out of north Cambridgeshire. Over the course of his thirty years "in the business", he has worked with the likes of Tony Hadley, Donovan, Flock of Seagulls and Meatloaf to create some of the most thought-provoking (and foot-tapping) music on the avant-folk scene. He is a regular feature at the Cambridge Folk Festival and has appeared on BBC Radio 3. *Avant-Folk Magazine* recently voted him one of the sixteen most influential solo acoustic musicians in the south of England. His new album *The Naked Presidents (Vol. 1)* has been well received and is available from <u>his website</u>.

Music

The Naked Presidents (Vol. 1)　　　　　[Vannity, 2007]
Up And Around With Maurice Vanns　　　[Vannity, 2005]
Never A Dull Moment – Duets And Tributes [Epistle Music, 1981]
Journeys In Time And Thought　　　　　[Epistle Music, 1979]
Vanns Full Of Love　　　　　　　　　[Epistle Music,1977]
The Sad Tale Of Neville Devil　　　　　[Epistle Music, 1976]

[more]

Other Work

Avant-Folk Magazine (ed. 2005 – present)
Painting All The Passports Brown   [Vannity Books, 2006]
Full Of Love: The Maurice Vanns Story [Vannity Books, 2005]

News

01/11/07 – The latest issue of *Avant-Folk* is out now! To order a copy, visit <u>my website</u> or, if you're a subscriber, it should already be winging its way to you. Many thanks for all your support, friends. I'll see you at the Lion's Mane in three weeks!

30/10/07 – Just a reminder that there are limited places at the Lion's Mane gig on the 22nd, so let me know in advance if you're coming. For more details, visit <u>my website</u>.

09/10/07 – I've just finished demoing a few songs that might make it onto *TNP (Vol. 2)*. Sounding pretty good! If you're lucky, I might play a few on the 22nd. Feel free to drop me an <u>e-mail</u> if you're planning on turning up.

06/10/07 – BREAKING NEWS! I've confirmed a booking for the Lion's Mane pub in Haverhill on the 22nd of November. I'll let you know as and when the rest of the tour fills up.

28/09/07 – Happy birthday me! Many thanks for all your e-mails and e-cards. The new songs are going well and that's the best gift I could ever ask for. Also, I bought myself a digital watch.

23/09/07 – Just to let you know, I'm going to be booking a huge nationwide tour for this winter. I'll be posting details on <u>my website</u> as and when they're confirmed. Should be loads of dates – very exciting! Watch this space!

<u>[more]</u>

From: s.ackland@alton-associates.co.uk
To: altonUK@alton-associates.co.uk
Subject: Stapler

Message:

Still no luck on the stapler front. Mike – the kitchen
on the mezzanine level didn't yield any results either.
You said there were five or six in a drawer there, are
you sure? Was it perhaps somewhere else?

All best,

Sandra

This e-mail and any files transmitted with it are private
and intended solely for the use of the individual or
entity to whom they are addressed. If you are not the
intended recipient, please notify admin-mail@alton-
associates.co.uk with "Incorrect Delivery Of Internal
Message" in the subject line along with the exact date
and time you received this message.

All e-mail data may be stored and monitored for the
purposes of security, training and blackmail.

16:15

...NEW SURVEY SUGGESTS THAT 80% OF OFFICE WORKERS GET DISTRACTED TOO EASILY...PARIS HILTON QUESTIONS WHETHER SHE IS NEWSWORTHY... UN CONSIDERS NUCLEAR ACTION...

24NEWS
*Providing news 24 hours a day
in increasingly unnecessary places*

From: s.ackland@alton-associates.co.uk
To: altonUK@alton-associates.co.uk
Subject: Stapler

Message:

Jeremy – I checked the delivery bay – no joy. I must
admit I did think it strange that Alton would be
receiving an order of 300 staplers. Though it would be
helpful for me if they did :-)

Any other suggestions dear colleagues. Time is running
out!! These documents won't staple themselves. I'll
staple them. But I do need a stapler. Has nobody got one
at all?

All best,

S

This e-mail and any files transmitted with it are private
and intended solely for the use of the individual or
entity to whom they are addressed. If you are not the
intended recipient, please notify admin-mail@alton-
associates.co.uk with "Incorrect Delivery Of Internal
Message" in the subject line along with the exact date
and time you received this message.

All e-mail data may be stored and monitored for the
purposes of security, training and blackmail.

From: dconnolly@alton-associates.co.uk
To: ac31-team4-group@alton-associates.co.uk
Subject: Re: Knees Up!

Message:

Hi again,

Look, I just got an e-mail from Suz. She wants to tell
you all that her and Dan are NOT going away together
this weekend. Actually she's going home because her mum
is dying of cancer. Seems like I put my foot in it a
bit, so sorry for that.

D

This e-mail and any files transmitted with it are private
and intended solely for the use of the individual or
entity to whom they are addressed. If you are not the
intended recipient, please notify admin-mail@alton-
associates.co.uk with "Incorrect Delivery Of Internal
Message" in the subject line along with the exact date
and time you received this message.

All e-mail data may be stored and monitored for the
purposes of security, training and blackmail.

From: s.ackland@alton-associates.co.uk
To: altonUK@alton-associates.co.uk
Subject: Stapler

Message:

Hi all. Mike has suggested that I check the 3rd floor
men's loo. It's a long shot, but he was adamant that
I'd find what I was looking for there. Only problem is
I am a woman and therefore forbidden to enter. Any men
out there able to help me out? Mike says he's too busy.
I'm running out of time. I really need to staple these
documents.

S

This e-mail and any files transmitted with it are private
and intended solely for the use of the individual or
entity to whom they are addressed. If you are not the
intended recipient, please notify admin-mail@alton-
associates.co.uk with "Incorrect Delivery Of Internal
Message" in the subject line along with the exact date
and time you received this message.

All e-mail data may be stored and monitored for the
purposes of security, training and blackmail.

From: s.ackland@alton-associates.co.uk
To: altonUK@alton-associates.co.uk
Subject: Stapler

Message:

Dear All,

Well it seems like I've been the victim of a very cruel
prank. I've wasted two hours looking for a stapler in
places where there were no staplers at all. I suppose
you all think this is very funny.

I have now found a stapler no thanks to you! Sheila who
sits opposite me had one. But joking aside - does anyone
have any staples?

All best,

Sandra

This e-mail and any files transmitted with it are private
and intended solely for the use of the individual or
entity to whom they are addressed. If you are not the
intended recipient, please notify admin-mail@alton-
associates.co.uk with "Incorrect Delivery Of Internal
Message" in the subject line along with the exact date
and time you received this message.

All e-mail data may be stored and monitored for the
purposes of security, training and blackmail.

From: j.kemp@alton-associates.co.uk
To: salesgroup2@alton-associates.co.uk
Subject: Brahms

Message:

Who walked my dog?

Brahms is not supposed to be doing any exercise until
he recovers from his operation. But when I was at my 4
o'clock meeting someone walked him, despite the note
clearly stapled to his back. He's not in a good way.
Please come forward so I can report you to the RSPCA.

Jenny

This e-mail and any files transmitted with it are private
and intended solely for the use of the individual or
entity to whom they are addressed. If you are not the
intended recipient, please notify admin-mail@alton-
associates.co.uk with "Incorrect Delivery Of Internal
Message" in the subject line along with the exact date
and time you received this message.

All e-mail data may be stored and monitored for the
purposes of security, training and blackmail.

System Log Out

This computer (including the software installed on it, files stored on its hard drive and any websites it has been used to view) is the exclusive property of Alton Associates UK Ltd, a subsidiary of Anceps International. All data is confidential and employees are bound by law to refer to Alton Associates (and any other company in the Anceps family) only in a positive light. All data may be recorded, monitored, analysed and used against you in a court of law. Any words added to the custom dictionary are now the sole property of Anceps International and their copyright will be enforced accordingly.

Log Out   Cancel

HAIR INTERROGATION

Cut Up isn't a salon; it's a lifestyle birth-right. And a salon.
Cut Up's hair creator-gods don't just cut and style hair –
they fuck it up.

Limited appointments available
with Hair Kaiser Freddie P.

CORE SERVICES	JUNIOR CG	SENIOR CG
Hanging out (1 hour)	£20	£40
Hanging out (2 hours)	£25	£50
Comb through with oil	£30	£100
Someone else's haircut	£60	£220
Original haircut (0–300 hairs cut)	£123.50	£500
Original haircut (300–500 hairs cut)	£200	£650
Original haircut (500+ hairs cut)	ASK	ASK

The above with Kaiser – multiply Senior CG price by 2.6

OPTIONAL EXTRAS

Wardrobe integration	£24	£40
Relationship guidance	ASK	ASK
Sarcasm	£45	FREE
Pete Doherty	ASK	don't ASK

Cut Up isn't like other salons. Creativity is valued above all else,
so none of our CGs have been 'trained'.

He Doesn't Know He Wants You... But He Does (Want You)!

There are no two ways about it – finding a good man is hard. But what's even harder is what comes after you've found him – getting him! You certainly need a few tricks up your sleeve, and after reading this article you will have (those tricks up your sleeve). You see, it's all very well "chatting" and "bonding", but if you're going to snag the hunk of your dreams, you need to use a little bit of science – the science of body language.

You might not think it, but body language accounts for more than 96% of everyday communication. Your mouth may be saying, "Milk and no sugar please", but your body language is screaming, "BISCUIT BISCUIT BISCUIT BISCUIT!" (if, for example, you are being offered a cup of tea and you really want a biscuit). The twitches of your eyebrows, the movements of your hands, the way you're standing – it's like a secret code, and most of the time, you don't even know you're doing it. But if you can understand and control your body language, you can use it to your advantage.

Top Tips

The most important thing to communicate is that you're interested in him, but not desperate. Try a few of the following:

- Gently brush against his shoulders with your hands as often as possible.

- Play with your hair (but not too much).

- Laugh at everything. If he's not already talking to you, ask his name, then laugh.

- Get your face as close to his face as you can. If this is proving difficult, try faking a stumble or inner-ear problem.

- Align your crotch with his – this suggests the possibility of sex.

- Rock back and forth slightly and make little moaning noises.

- Maintain eye contact at all times. If this means walking into a door, do it – you will appear vulnerable. But try not to bleed – men hate blood.

Remember, body language is a powerful tool, and it only takes a small mistake to give off all the wrong signals, so be careful. If you find yourself turning away from the man you're after, breaking eye contact or walking slowly backwards with your hands in front of your face, the chances are you're giving off negative signals. Above all else, remember to relax. Be yourself and let your personality shine through. Unless you've got a terrible personality, in which case don't be yourself. Be someone else. Perhaps Cat Deeley.

So next time you're at a party, don't panic! With just a little confidence and a lot of self-conscious pseudo-psychological manipulation, you can give yourself the illusion of adequacy you desperately need just to keep afloat in a cruel and lonely world. Either that or just get really, really drunk.

Time to start "stocking" up!

So, with just a few weeks of the year to go, Christmas is nearly upon us again. There's no need to panic over presents, though – here at Garment Shack, we've got the perfect selection of gifts for all ages. Just look at our incredible range of pastel fleeces, all quality-assured and all half-price for this month only. With prices this good, you might just be tempted to get one for yourself as well!

Don't miss our sensational 3-in-1 jackets, the perfect choice for any season. Wear the inner as a snug fleece, the outer as a waterproof coat or both together for the ultimate outdoor clothing experience. With that kind of versatility, this really is the only coat you'll ever need. If you don't believe me, just look at the models in the photo. The man – let's call him Stephen – is so happy with his fleecy inner that he's actually laughing. That's the kind of comfort we're talking here. And the woman – let's call her Penny – is so well protected from the elements by her waterproof outer that she seems to be experiencing a degree of pleasure that borders on indecent. Look at the way she's throwing her head back in ecstasy and gripping Stephen's hand so tightly. There might even be a hint of fear on his face, so extreme is her delight in the waterproof properties of her garment.

If you're after something a bit lighter, you can't do better than our Long Sleeve Scoop Neck Tops. Available in Teal, Mulberry, Fudge and Conker, these simple yet versatile garments are perfect as a gift for a sophisticated, fashion-conscious woman. They might be the kind of thing that Stephen would buy for Penny – just as a surprise, just because he knows she would like it. It wouldn't need to be a special occasion. Sometimes he buys her little presents just because he wants to. Not always Long Sleeve Scoop Neck Tops. No, sometimes it's something a little more intimate, a little more exciting. Lustrous Bootcut Velvet Trousers in Amethyst or Shale, for example, or a stylish Argyle Jumper which she would wear last thing at night, curled up in front of the fire with a glass of brandy. Seeing her so warm, relaxed and appropriately clothed, he might silently kneel behind her and breathe in the scent of her perfume before letting his hands slide gently under the double-stitched ribbed hem of her pure cotton, machine-washable sweater. She will sigh lightly and lean back into him, feeling the rough texture of his hard-wearing Pleat Front Cords against her. Then they melt into one another's arms, letting their high-quality, tumble-drier-friendly garments fall to the floor, and breathlessly, tenderly consummate their love, neither of them speaking a word, not even to comment on our great prices or twenty-eight-day no-quibble guarantee.

Stephen Matterling
Garment Shack Managing Director

I Traced Back My Family That I'm Descended From

Deborah Jacques didn't know what to expect when she started tracing her family tree, but she was certainly surprised by what she found. "It took me completely unawares," she told us. "I never knew that I had relatives in the farmyard!" You see, when Deborah traced her family tree, she found more than just names and dates – she found breeds, weights and prices at auction!

"When I started this hobby," Deborah reveals, "I was hoping I'd find blue blood – a princess or countess or queen or something. My grandmother had just died, and I'd recently found out that my son was gay, so I thought I'd better do my bit to keep the family together." With the help of professional experts at the family tree website, GenealogyInABottle. com, she started to investigate the history of her family. "At first, it was all quite normal," she told us. "I found out that my dad's side of the family came from Scotland and used to work in the factories in Edinburgh, and that my Mum's side had been in the Essex area for generations. But when I got back to my great-great-grandparents' parents, instead of a name on the birth records, there was just a Best In Breed certificate. I was amazed!"

The boffins at GenealogyInABottle.com checked out her find and told her it was absolutely true – before they'd settled down as farmers and factory workers, Deborah's ancestors had been prize-winning Wessex Saddlebacks. "I've always tried to keep myself trim," joked Deborah, "so it was a shock to find that I come from a family who are real porkers." Almost the next day, Deborah contacted the British Pig Association, but they didn't want to hear about it. "They didn't want to hear about it," Deborah confided in us. "I told them I should be in their catalogue of rare breeds, but they just hung up on me. I don't think they're used to getting a phone call from an actual pig! And I was crying a bit, so they might not have been able to hear me."

For weeks afterwards, Deborah took to wearing a T-shirt saying, "I AM A PIG" with a slogan on the back adding, "NO, REALLY. AN ACTUAL PIG."

Tree And Found Out
A Long Line . . .
OF PIGS!

She had five of the T-shirts specially made in different colours so that she could wear one every day. "She's a real joker," her friend Karen told us. "She always likes to have a laugh at her own expense. It was the same when her husband left. I've still got one of those 'LONELY FAILURE' T-shirts somewhere. I saved it so we could have a laugh about it in a few years. I'll have to try and get hold of one of the pig ones too – I could start a collection!"

But it's not just T-shirts Deborah's got planned. Discovering this pork skeleton in her family's closet has spurred Deborah on to get the plastic surgery she's always wanted. "Discovering this pork skeleton in my family's closet has spurred me on to get the plastic surgery I've always wanted," Deborah revealed. "I always knew there was something wrong with my nose, and now I know what it is. I've got a stupid ugly pig face with a stupid ugly pig nose. But now I can fix it. I don't have to be a pig any more. I don't have to be ugly my whole life. This explains it all and I can fix it. I can make everything better.

No wonder Stewart never fancied girls, when his own mother had a huge ugly pig face. Maybe this will help him. I just want to help my boy."

For now, though, Deborah's got a lot on her plate (or should that be "in her trough"!?). With appearances on television's *Weird Or What?* and interviews in national newspapers, offers of work are rolling in. There's even the possibility that she'll feature in the new television adverts for GenealogyInABottle.com, which will be shown nationwide next year. After all, without GenealogyInABottle.com (quote PIG WOMAN for 10% discount), she'd never have known about Great-Great-Great-Grandma Bessie in the first place. So, what are her plans for the future? "I just need to get together the money for the surgery," she told us, "then it'll all be okay." And will she manage it? You bet she SWILL!

Party Panic!

We've all been there – you've squeezed into your LBD, checked for VPL, booked a BMW and stocked up on MDMA, then, just minutes before the biggest party of your life, something goes horribly wrong. It's at times like this that you have to prove yourself. Be resourceful! Think quick! Take our multiple-choice quiz!

Digestive Disaster

Just before you walk out of the door, you feel a strange pain in your stomach. Before you know what's happening, you have to rush to the toilet and start having the worst diarrhoea attack of your life.
Do you…

a) Cancel the cab and prepare for a long night in the smallest room.

b) Go to the party anyway – the more often you visit the toilet, the more drugs it'll look like you're doing.

c) Search the attic for that adult-sized nappy your ex bought you as a joke.

d) Use *Gastrapax All-In-One Digestive Treatment Caplets* for 24-hour protection and confidence, then dance the night away safe in the knowledge that Gastrapax offers fast and effective relief from diarrhoea.

Weather Worries

You've managed to leave the house, but the downpour outside is like stepping into a cold shower.
Do you…

a) Wear your huge yellow waterproof and risk looking like a walking marquee.

b) Duck under a passing stranger's umbrella – maybe you'll get on really well.

c) Forget the party, strip down to your underwear and dance wildly in the rain.

d) Use *Gastrapax All-In-One Digestive Treatment Caplets* for fast-acting, reliable results, safe in the knowledge that they are accredited by the British Gastrology Council and the Centre For Digestive Health.

Conversation Crisis

You're finally at the party and it's going swimmingly. You get talking to a guy who seems interested in you and even better – he's gorgeous! But then he mentions that he's going through a messy divorce. Do you . . .

a) Back off – best not to get involved in a nasty situation.

b) Ask for his ex-wife's name and address before playfully offering to have her killed.

c) Blurt out, "Yeah, well I'm married anyway."

d) Look crestfallen and sigh gently as you let your eyes sink to the floor, as if imagining what could have been in another life, another time. Then, let your hand slide gently into your bag and pull out your **Gastrapax All-In-One Digestive Treatment Caplets**. Look up with a shy half-smile and a glimmer of hope in your eyes as you nervously offer him one. As he takes it, brush your hair away from your eyes and raise a caplet to your mouth. Swallow it as he swallows his and stare lovingly into his eyes as, together, the two of you experience effective and long-lasting relief from diarrhoea, bloating and over three hundred related bowel disorders.

If you answered mostly A:
You're so boring that even your closest friends secretly hate you. When you were born, your mother took one look at your stupid, boring face and screamed for the midwife to push you back in. All these years later, everyone wishes she had, or, failing that, just strangled you with the umbilical cord. Anything to prevent the world from having to put up with your mind-numbingly tedious existence. There's no way back from here. You've got to the point where even your suicide would be boring. Your worthless life is like the constant stream of watery faeces that only **Gastrapax All-In-One Digestive Treatment Caplets** can rid you of.

If you answered mostly B:
You're the life and soul of the party, and possibly other bits of it as well, like the spleen and the oesophagus. You're the one everyone comes to for advice on their career, their love life and the condition of their lower intestine. Don't let them down – point them in the direction of **Gastrapax All-In-One Digestive Treatment Caplets**.

If you answered mostly C:
Martha, your parents miss you. All they want is for you to be safe. Please, please come home.

If you answered mostly D:
You're the kind of hip and happening chick who knows what she wants and knows how to get it. You should consider a career in marketing – there are plenty of large, Birmingham-based pharmaceutical companies that would be glad of your services.

Gastrapax All-In-One Digestive Treatment Caplets should not be taken recreationally. If symptoms persist, consult your GP. If your GP starts going on about the long-term health risks of addiction to phenol-based gastric medicines, try taking even more Gastrapax.

FUDGE MAG

Style, music, creative arts, clubs and shit...

This Month...

GAY BIRD WATCHING

BO! & TING

DESIGNER DRUGS FOR KIDS

KATIE MELUA

SEXY PERIOD PANTS

Literally Da Bomb: THE BASRA CLUB SCENE

Forget the Yanks in Baghdad, it's classy British ex-pat action all the way. We tell you where to be seen, what to be seen in, and how to exploit the curfew.

Presenting the

Xi® *H5*
SPECIAL EDITION

The H5 has always been our most popular handset. Perhaps it's the sleek, futuristic design; perhaps it's the high-definition polymegapixel camera; perhaps it's the fact that it comes free with **Clear**® contracts – whatever the reason, the H5 has been a classic from the day it was born.

But here at **Xi**®, we're not content with just being the best. That's why we've developed the H5 SPECIAL EDITION, featuring an additional megapixel, variable levels of backlighting, 40% more sleekness, a total of eight blueteeth and a limited edition **Xi**® carrycase.

Best of all, the H5 SPECIAL EDITION has a surprise hidden inside it: four retractable multirange surround sound speakers. Just hit the ergonomically positioned trigger and these speakers will spring out of the phone and into action. You can use them to have conversations, listen to music or simply pump up the volume on your favourite **Xi**® ringtones.

With their revolutionary "bass attack" technology the Retractaphones™ let you get the party started wherever you are. On the train, in the cinema, at a memorial service – the possibilities are endless.

In the time of the world's beginning, there was a mighty elephant named Hashra. His tusks were made of polished jade and shone like the moon. The followers of Hashra lived in the forest beside the mountain and worshipped him every hour of the day. When a famine came upon their land, they prayed to Hashra to help them. They chanted his many names and lit the sacrificial fires. After a time, he appeared to them, but the famine did not end. After all, he was an elephant, not an agricultural consultant. He probably trampled all the crops and made things worse, if anything.

Hindu Folktale

If you could talk to anyone, anywhere, any time, just imagine the stories they'd tell . . .

Clear®
You're In Ambitious Hands™

The Sketch
Notes on Today's Parliamentary Notables by Simon Dell

Bang! Whoosh! Bang! The fireworks were flying all round Westminster yesterday. "Ooh" and "Aaah" we all repeated on command like excitable six-year-olds, awaiting our sparklers so we could spell out rude words in the air.

"It's not a question of what the Prime Minister wants to do," came the boom of the opposition leader like a rocket blasting out blue bulbs of light across the dark political sky, "it's a question of what he hasn't yet done." It was the use of the word "question" I liked best. He used it twice. Very clever, I thought, very clever indeed. I quipped to my esteemed colleague from The Diplomat that this had been rather clever, and he smiled at me.

Next, it was the beleaguered PM himself, like a Roman candle in the wind, with his reply – "I doubt you could do any better" – going off like a rocket that makes a farting noise as it takes off but only pops lightly in the air at the end. His chancellor didn't offer the best support. Like a traffic light, he seemed to keep changing his mind. "I offer my unconditional support" became "I have commissioned a review of our policy on this matter." Oh dear, we thought, time to have some piping hot soup from Mrs Speaker's stall and get ready for the Catherine Wheel.

Talking of which, the Foreign Secretary didn't disappoint, her whirling frenzy of policy review enough to confound the shadows for a few minutes until she predictably ground to a halt. The Catherine Wheel is the closest a woman gets to feeling what sex is like for a man, I quipped to my colleague from The Diplomat, but I'm not sure he heard me, such was the commotion.

After the Catherine Wheel, the adventure lost direction slightly. MPs ran off in different directions to meet friends from school and us journalists were left to thrash it out near the goal posts. "Aren't tropes fantastic?" I quipped to my colleague from The Diplomat, but he had gone.

Order was restored when someone said it was time to put the guy on the bonfire. There was some argument about who got to light the pyre but in the end the leader of the opposition did so with a match made from recycled wood. "We're more green than you," heckled he. The PM looked dejected, no doubt recalling the old maxim: "Remember, remember the fifth of November – carbon emissions or not."

I fell asleep in the car on the way home. It was the best fireworks night ever!

Noughts & Crosses *John Osborne*

This week saw the first round of the ISCL World Championship, and what a week it's been. The long-awaited rematch between world number three Inra Mahmud and rising star Laos McKinney provided quite a spectacle for the gathered crowds. An opening flurry of textbook geometric reasoning from Mahmud was weathered, if not seen off, by the plucky Hebridean's use of a perpendicular defence rarely seen on the professional circuit. McKinney swiftly followed this with a thrusting horizontal gambit and, while the world number three was reeling from this (possibly remembering the trauma of last year's near-defeat by Polto, who employed similar tactics in the final set), he initiated a tactical play based on what promised to be a complex series of iterative differentials. However, the veteran Syrian's experience shone through as he allowed the onslaught to wash over him before striking back along the obverse diagonal. In the end, it was McKinney's incomplete grasp of topology that cost him the win, allowing the game to be drawn and robbing us of what could have been a stunning upset at this early stage.

Meanwhile, the much-fancied outsider Keith Danger was drawn against aging ex-champ Peter Goblov. Danger, a twenty-eight-year-old graphologist from Sussex, bore up well under the pressure of Goblov's trademark sequential attack, fighting back with an alternating high-low approach and eventually forcing the draw.

Weatherman vs. Rodriguez also finished in a tied game, as did the Stapleton–Roe match, which was played simultaneously. Benling–Deably, Urqat–Funk and Habermaier–Ruit all finished with the players level on points. Soning held Paddleforth to a hotly contested no-score draw, while Bulton vs. Fletch finished nil-nil. In group F, The Achan–Yop match was declared null after a seven hour stalemate and Hicks vs. Sutherland has been postponed until the seventeenth.

The draw for the next round will take place on Tuesday.

Killing Your Mind (Do You Mind?)
The Friendly Bombs

Listening to the new EP by The Friendly Bombs is a bit like having a coffee enema, but through your eyes, and it isn't coffee, it's pure monkey semen scraped off the walls of a Warholesque brothel designed by a team of MC Eschers created in a secret lab by Hitler's evil twin whilst coming down off a thirteen-month crack binge. I liked it.

★★★★

I Love You
The Fags

Writing 100 words about a song by The Fags is a bit like being asked to write 1,000 words on an album by The Fags. 'I Love You' has an intricate simplicity that demands at least 120–130 words. I know journalists, good journalists, educated, decent, creative people with a passion for words and music that surpasses the passion for words and music held by lesser journalists, who have walked out of magazine offices up and down the capital upon being asked to write anything less than 100 words on a song by The Fags. 'The Fags deserve better!' they cried. I for one agree.

★★★★★

Symphony For The Departed
Serotonin Seraphim

Serotonin Seraphim are the fifth most important band making orchestral-clout-punk in the Dorking area, and 'Symphony For The Departed' is the eagerly awaited sixth single from their debut digital album *Ellipsis*. Anyone who already owns a copy of *Ellipsis*, or perhaps has a copy of this song as the b-side to 'Requiem For Love' or on one of the two live albums *Seraphim Fuck!* and *Live at the Roundhouse*, or who has perhaps seen the video on heavy rotation on MTV2, or downloaded the reggae remix on their mobiles last month as part of the Live Cancer promotion, will know that it's actually not all that.

★★

Last Night's Television (*with Simon Barker*)

My melancholic life in front of Logie Baird's insipid instrument of torture continues, my sofa a bed of thorns, the remote another nail. Last night, the wisdom of the programmers bestowed upon the humble television-watcher nothing out of the wretched ordinary as I found myself subjected to the horrifying emotional instability of character that is popularly known as Jodie Spencer, *Diddlesbury Close*'s least inspired blonde ditz. In plotting terms, the episode was less sophisticated than the contents of my six-month-old son's nappy. The accompanying press release (yes, they actually send out a press release for every episode) describes it as "a fast-paced comic episode that brings to light some of the serious realities of drug abuse". I found it slow, dull and obvious, with "comic moments" as subtle as gastroenteritis and about half as enjoyable.

The producers of *Diddlesbury Close* are not the only ones deluded enough to continue making an effort, it seems. Channel 4's season of thoughtful documentaries with cruel titles continues with a chin-stroking car-crash entitled *Dead Childish* – the tale of a couple who refused to accept the miscarriage of their second child and have instead carried on as normal: hiring a room in a private hospital for the "birth", buying baby clothes, decorating a nursery and instructing their understandably distraught five-year-old, Harry, to play with his baby sister. The show is horrifying to the point of hysteria as the couple, Peter and Jenny Walberry, put on an elaborate mime act for most of this gut-wrenching documentary, inviting the camera operators to hold their "invisible" baby girl, Sarah. Their delusion is developed to the point that they even attempt to explain the lack of physical evidence for their offspring. "Our little girl was born without a body," explains Jenny, grimacing. "The doctors say it's very rare," Peter chimes in, almost proudly. The documentary makers get their show-stopping ending as Social Services turn up to take Harry away and Peter and Jenny are delivered to a nearby psychiatric hospital, but by that point you might have already turned over to catch scary Scientologist and even scarier actor Pete McMann make his second appearance as FBI agent Ashley Stokes in *Armageddon II – This Time It's Really Over*. I saw this film at the cinema back when I was a film critic and all I can say is advert breaks really improve it, though not enough to stave off my compulsive desire to end it all on an almost nightly basis.

Freddie Lindsal wears *Il Lione* boots . . .

. . . because we pay him to.

Il Lione®
It means lion . . . in Italian™

You wouldn't steal a car.

You wouldn't embezzle
£10,000,000.

You wouldn't break into a
pensioner's flat and shit
all over her Princess Diana
commemorative crockery.

So why haven't you
got a TV licence?

If you don't have a TV licence, we'll catch you. You mark my words, sunshine, we'll catch you. And be warned, we are not nice people – in fact, we're quite nasty as it happens and you don't want us on your case – we're an 'eadache, mate. You don't need the 'assle – you get me? Just toddle off to the post office and fill in the green form like a good little boy – before someone gets hurt . . . bad.

The TV LICENCE Posse –
leave it out

The clouds are dark, the air is dark,
The seas and skies and lands are dark;
The rocks and trees and grass and soil,
The sons and daughters, old and young,
The fish and birds and snakes and sheep,
The darkness is upon them all.
The hand is dark, the foot is dark,
The corner of my hut is dark,
The pen and paper both are dark;
It's actually getting quite hard to see what I'm writing.

Traditional Maori Song

*If you could talk to anyone, anywhere, any time,
just imagine the stories they'd tell . . .*

Clear®
You're In Ambitious Hands™

THE News

Everyone loves **The News**!! Oi! Oi!

Win School Days Disco Tickets!! Page 12

Laura's sauciest Page 3 Pics yet – Naughty Schoolgirl Action!!

ROT IN HELL

Hayes convicted of Samantha Murder

Minging child killer Toby Hayes was jailed today for the murder of little Samantha Keeble. Before banging sicko Hayes up for life, the Judge at the old Bailey said: "My words are going to be printed in the newspapers tomorrow, so I'm going to hyperbolise."

There were cheers inside the court as the horrible pus-bag was sent down. As the verdict was read out, Samantha's parents,

Parents favourite to win Top Talent Search

currently taking part in TV's Top Talent Search, embraced each other and had a good old snog.

Outside the Old Bailey, the couple posed in costume for the crowds and made cheeky gestures towards the throng of photographers and journalists. Mrs Keeble made a passionate appeal to fans to vote for them in tonight's final of TV's Top Talent Search. "We really want to

There's sport on the back!

win," she said. Mr Keeble did his now trade-mark Ali G impression adding "booyakasha!" William Hill has them as 9-2 joint favourites with Sarah Dalton, the pint-sized bulimic from Basildon.

In press rooms up and down the UK calls were immediately made for another horrifying child murder case to help sell newspapers in what will undoubtedly be a time for national mourning.
(Turn to page 2!)

FORM FILLER?

6.00 a.m.	wake up
6.30 a.m.	brush teeth
7.00 a.m.	breakfast
7.30 a.m.	train to work
8.00 a.m.	read paper
8.30 a.m.	start work
9.00 a.m.	fill in forms
9.30 a.m.	fill in forms
10.00 a.m.	fill in forms
10.30 a.m.	fill in forms
11.00 a.m.	coffee break
11.30 a.m.	fill in forms
12:00 p.m.	torture locals
12.30 p.m.	fill in forms
1.00 p.m.	lunch
1.30 p.m.	browse shops
2.00 p.m.	stamp forms

OR TRAINED KILLER?

6.00 a.m.	killing
6.30 a.m.	killing
7.00 a.m.	breakfast
7.30 a.m.	killing
8.00 a.m.	mock locals
8.30 a.m.	killing
9.00 a.m.	climbing over logs
9.30 a.m.	killing
10.00 a.m.	killing
10.30 a.m.	killing
11.00 a.m.	coffee break
11.30 a.m.	killing
12.00 p.m.	torture locals
12.30 p.m.	killing
1.00 p.m.	lunch
1.30 p.m.	killing
2.00 p.m.	killing

CHANGE YOUR SCHEDULE

THE ARMY

WWW.FORMFILLERTOTRAINEDKILLER.ORG

JUV-FRO – MIRACLE HAIR STUFF

"My hair grew uncontrollably!"

Graham Jacobs – GB rowing star (4th, coxless pairs, Seoul Olympics/ 5th, coxless pairs, Atlanta Olympics) – uses new JUV-Fro to rejuvenate bald spots.

"I used to be fairly hairless. It didn't seem to matter when I was competing, but when all that finished my life fell apart."

JUV-Fro helped Britain's best-loved nearly-man reclaim his life (and hair) and it can help you too.

"People don't recognise me any more, which helps."

To experience the benefits of JUV-Fro's miracle, natural* hair growth formula send a blank cheque and a stamped self-addressed envelope to: JUV-Fro, PO Box 234, Swindon, SW1 1ZZ

* 12% natural products used throughout our range.

Peter Redwood – *He's thinking what you're all saying*

A Load of Old Humbug

Leftist do-gooders in Cornwall are trying to ban one of the area's oldest Christmas traditions. **Labour councillors** have cancelled the annual 'Running of the Raghead' event in St Davids, north Cornwall, in case it **"offends Muslims"**. Just another case of political correctness gone mad! These secular spoilsports will not stop until Christmas has been well and truly **eradicated**!

Decent British people in Cornwall are naturally **OUTRAGED** at the actions of the short-sighted councillors. Miriam McGaskel, 82, said: "For me, Christmas has always been about love and family. The violent pursuit of Arabs through the local streets has always added to this."

Jim Reid, 42, who runs the local post office, was **INCENSED**: "This is just another case of prejudice against Christians by secular devil-worshippers. We're the ones being persecuted, not these so-called **asylum seekers**."

Even angel-faced, small, naive children can see that the **idiotic** counsellors are **idiotic**. 12-year-old James Radcliffe said: "It's stupid because it's not like we use a real Muslim, it's normally just a village lad wearing boot polish and that."

I can't say I'm surprised. It's just the latest in a long line of **mean-spirited** gestures by the bunch of Scrooges that run this country. Last year in Birmingham, councillors stopped picturesque, tiny, inexperienced children from sending Christmas cards to each other, just because they personally didn't like some of the slogans printed on the cards. Any **decent**, **right-thinking** person knows that a phrase like "Nig-Nogs roasting on an open fire" is just a bit of **harmless fun**.

Then there was the time in Bradford a group of polite, frail, old grannies who had **fought Nazis** in the War were stopped from singing traditional hymns just because they had the word "Paki" in them, which wasn't even offensive when the hymns were written.

This country is **going to the dogs**, placing a bet on a **foreign** dog that's clearly got fleas and then crowing on about "equality" as the dog leaves the race track, straps a **bomb** to its back and blows up good-looking, istsy-bitsy-teeny-weeny, child-like children.

I'd say "Happy Christmas", but I'd probably get arrested by the **Thought Police**. And it's still November.

CLEAR: Hey buddy!
For the next
fortnight only,
we're giving away
(for free!) eight
thousand BigChat
rewards to Clear
customers. To
qualify, all you
need to do is make
100 hours of calls
over the next week,
then txt 'BIGCHAT'
to 100345 and you
could be randomly
selected to win
an MP3 player (or
promotional pen).

PENALTY FARES

If you cannot produce on demand a valid ticket for your entire journey, you may be liable to a fine of £2,500 or the price of a first-class single to your destination (whichever is greater).

PRIVIRAIL

CRIPPLED BY DEBT?

Gutted! New Standard Bank does not give a damn! Why should we? We've looked after our money. Why should we help you out just because you can't keep your wallet in your trousers for more than thirty seconds at a time? You didn't see us queuing outside Habitat on 8 a.m. Boxing Day to buy a three-piece suite we couldn't afford. We haven't got an "All Le Creuset" kitchen. We're not members of a gym we never go to. We haven't decided "It's time I got into art collecting." We don't have Ocado on speed dial. We don't go to Hay-on-Wye every year. We're not thinking of moving the whole family over to France for a "better life". We don't drive an Espace. Our kids don't wear Petit Bateau. Nor are we going to encourage them to take out student loans on top of their £200 "spending money" a week. There is nothing big or clever about getting into debt. Nothing. If you can't afford something, don't have it. You are not so special that you can have everything you clap your pathetic materialistic eyes on. You make us sick.

All right, then. Seeing as you feel totally worthless now, we'll let you have some money. But just you wait till you see the terms and conditions. They apply. Oh, they apply, all right.

NEW STANDARD
Complete and Utter Bankers

Classifieds – MEDIA

AROMA DIRECTOR
Brands 2 Go! – Communicating Perspicuously

Can you tell a fetor from a mephitis?

There's a funny smell in here and it's stopping us from communicating perspicuously. We're searching for a lively, intelligent Aroma Director to head up osmic research in our East London office.

You will have three years' experience, a degree in an aroma-related subject and the ability to work whilst being subjected to incredibly loud electro-pop.

Salary: £30–35 k

DEPUTY VICE DIRECTOR OF PODCASTING
Studio V – Branding The Dream

Podcasting's the new blogging, and blogging's still hot as shit. We need someone to do podcasts about life inside Studio V. We want to put something creative and fun back into the world by telling people about our table football set and sofas (yes, sofas! in an office!). Whatever happens we mustn't let on what complete wankers we are. It's called creativity. We're creative.

You will be creative, creatively minded, have a creative flair, with the ability to think creatively, follow instructions and live on £90 a week.

Wankers need not apply.

**EXECUTIVE DIRECTOR OF
ANYTHING YOU LIKE**
The Orange Grove – A Beautiful Place To Work

Over 50? Low competence levels? Shop in Laura Ashley?

We offer vanity positions to independently wealthy women who used to work in publishing but got passed over for promotion one too many times and decided "to hell with it all, let's just have a change." We can't offer a salary, but if you're looking for a business card and a place to come from 10 a.m. till 4 p.m. and talk about when you were at university with P. G. Wodehouse's grandson, then this beautiful place is for you. www.The-Orange-Grove.org.uk

---

Sir,

Why doesn't The Sentinel run a campaign? It doesn't matter what it's about. I just need something to alleviate this enormous burden of middle-class guilt.

In times of great need I always turn to The Sentinel. When all those people were dying of famine in that African country, your well-informed, empathetic reports helped to ease my conscience as I shopped organically for things I knew my anorexic daughter wouldn't touch. Likewise, when all those families were left homeless after that big storm on Boxing Day 2004, knowing you had a campaign going so other people could donate money made me feel a lot better about the old 4x4.

Yours truly,

John Rowe

Sir,

I am outraged about Essex. I thought we'd done away with it in the late eighties. I had no idea it was still going on, but then the other day I noticed it – squatting at the end of the A13 like a boorish vagrant doing a poo.

I'm baffled. Didn't we all agree on this? Essex is wrong. All those people walking around saying, "I've got loads of money!" It just won't do. No one's got any real money there anyway, and the ones who do don't know what to do with it. It's like the East End of London but without all those fabulous Jack the Ripper tours.

I've started my own campaign (seeing as that last one you ran against SUVs was pitiful) and I'd be glad if you could advertise it for me. If your readers want to get involved they should go to my web site: www.banessex.org.

Yours etc.,

Mrs J. Norfolk. JP

DADS!
The Oedipal complex is a choice. Spend that Christmas bonus wisely.

The Great Big Toy Shop

Because you probably should

STEPHEN PACK – A sports writer of this year
Asks the questions others were afraid to ask.

MILD-GATE SCANDAL

Why controversial new manager is the right choice

The chickens will always come home to roost and this week, Salford lad David Mild was installed as the new manager of Manchester United. After due consideration, the board put age before beauty and chose as their big cheese, their head honcho, their big gun, a man many had consigned to the scrapheap after he couldn't cut the mustard at relegation-bound Sheffield United. The chance of a lifetime, or an accident waiting to happen? Will champagne corks be popping as Mild bursts Chelsea's bubble, or has he bitten off more than he can chew? Will he come out firing on all cylinders, or be just another damp squib? Can you teach an old dog new tricks, or will Manchester United be another nail in the coffin of David Mild?

Only time will tell – but the undeniable truth is that Mild's appointment has put the cat amongst the pigeons in British football. Many were shocked at Manchester United chief executive Billy Barton's decision; he and Mild are like chalk and cheese, and there are plenty that think the Red Devils' boss is living in cloud-cuckoo-land, that Mild will just bite the hand that feeds him, that he is an abject failure who lacks the courage of his convictions and has no place among the crème-de-la-crème of football managers. Others, however, like his no-nonsense approach. Here is a man, they say, who is not afraid to call a spade a spade. They think that Mild is as good as it gets; that his troubles in Sheffield were a flash in the pan and that he'll rise from the ashes of the Bramall Lane days and bring home the bacon for United in the eleventh hour of the season.

And wouldn't that make Chelsea fans as sick as parrots? They've been running off into the distance all season, ahead by a country mile at one point. If Mild can turn United's fortunes around, West London will rue the day. But Mild has to push all the right buttons and nip any potential problems in the bud. No pain, no gain. He has to show Chelsea that there's no more mister nice guy and this is no laughing matter as he'll be doing it just in the nick of time. This is the acid test for Mild – but don't expect him to be all-singing, all-dancing. He'll not want to rock the boat at United – his view is that if it ain't broke, don't fix it. His "one for all and all for one" attitude will be the same as we've always seen from him. He'll promote his back-to-basics approach to the backroom staff at Old Trafford and, mark my words, they'll all be banging their heads together and getting back to the drawing board this week, before Saturday's landmark match against Chelsea.

The bottom line is that some are born great and I fully support Mild's appointment. Here is a man who laughs in the face of danger. When the chips are down, he rises to the occasion and has done sterling work when faced with many a close shave. To those who think he should have been avoided like the plague, I say: make no mistake, there is life in the old dog yet. The legendary David Mild will make and mend at Manchester United. He will lay it on the line to prove he is capable of life in the fast lane and his critics will be left without a leg to stand on as he snatches victory from the jaws of defeat and dedicates it to the late great Alex Ferguson. Chelsea have been resting on their laurels for time immemorial, their devil-may-care manager living the life of Riley, enjoying a life of luxury and proving a law unto himself. But it's a game of two halves and the glory days could well be over for Chelsea. With a consummate professional like Mild back in gainful employment, it could soon be game, set and match.

Mild and Manchester United – I think this could be the beginning of a beautiful friendship. I'll be waiting with bated breath. But that goes without saying.

Fenleys Supermarket

We check over 10,000 prices in other stores
every week, so you don't have to. Seriously.
Don't even bother going into those places.
There's just no need.

Fenleys Organic
Farmhouse Bloomer

INGREDIENTS: organic flour, organic water, really organic yeast, genuinely organic salt, definitely not flavouring E3340 or an artificial preservative agent derived from diesel.

WARNING! Do not allow product to come into contact with eyes, skin or children. In the event of ingestion and/or swallowing, do not induce vomiting or operate heavy machinery. GentleCare Family Pharmaceuticals (a division of Axis Chemicals International) is not liable for: (a.) pregnancy, heart defects or a nervous disposition (b.) almonds (c.) lack of enthusiasm, listlessness and general ennui or (d.) subsequent use of packaging as a makeshift percussion instrument. Not suitable for children underwater.

4098 214

This card may only be used by the authorised
signatory. If you forget your pin code, call 0800 0238
12647 and we'll tell you it. If you have stolen this card
and are thinking about using that to your advantage,
please do not. IT IS AGAINST THE LAW.

This card is the property of **Relax&Shop Ltd**. If it is
found please send to **Relax&Shop** PO 2386 Luton,
or give it to a friendly policeman or an employee of a
recognisable shop or business. Don't give it to a
beggar. We cannot stress that enough.

Relax&Shop is a
subsidiary of Passively
Consume PLC.

www.relax&shop.com

19:16

FENLEYS SUPERMARKET

DUNSTAN ROAD
TEL: 0854 001 831

WHLML BREAD	0.85
GARLIC (LOOSE) 2 @ 0.35	0.70
PROBIOTIC YOG X4	2.99
SMTHIE (PGNT/LNGS)	3.69
LOFAT SOYA MILK	0.96
CH TIK MICROMEAL	1.99

TOTAL	11.18
CASH	20.00
CHANGE DUE	8.82

YOU COULD HAVE EARNED 11,180 POINTS
WITH THIS TRANSACTION. BUT YOU DIDN'T.
INSTEAD, YOU LET THEM SLIP THROUGH YOUR
FINGERS LIKE SO MANY DEAD GOLDFISH
BECAUSE YOU'RE TOO PROUD TO SIGN UP FOR
THE LOYALTY CARD. JUST WHO DO YOU THINK
YOU ARE, ANYWAY? SOME KIND OF ANARCHIST?
LET'S NOT FORGET THAT YOU'RE STILL
SHOPPING AT A SUPERMARKET. JUST BECAUSE
YOU DON'T HAVE A LOYALTY CARD, YOU THINK
YOU'RE ABSOLVED OF ALL GUILT. WELL
LET ME TELL YOU SOMETHING, CHE GUEVARA
- YOU'RE GOING DOWN WITH THE REST OF US,
PRINCIPLES OR NO PRINCIPLES, AND THERE'S
NOTHING YOU CAN DO ABOUT IT.

THANK YOU FOR SHOPPING AT FENLEYS

YOU WERE SERVED BY **LEYSHA**, WHO LOOKED
AT YOUR BASKET AND DECIDED THAT YOU
WILL, IN ALL PROBABILITY, DIE ALONE AND
UNLOVED AND NO AMOUNT OF POMEGRANATE AND
LEMONGRASS SMOOTHIE CAN CHANGE THAT.

PLEASE RETAIN FOR FUTURE REFERENCE.

THANKYOU.

INSTRUCTIONS

- Rotate the stool until your face is inside the white circle on the screen.

- Insert £5 (coins accepted: 10p, 20p, 50p, £1, £2).

- Relax and wait for the flash.

- You will be shown the picture and given the option to re-take. You may re-take a maximum of 3 times.

- If you are dissatisfied with the photograph, try a different facial expression. Remember, looking too serious may make you come across as threatening.

- Don't smile too much either. It makes you look like a brain-damaged child. And don't give me any of that one-eyebrow-raised nonsense either.

- I'm sure there's something you can do.

- Did you not think to bring a comb, at the very least? Do you really want to spend the next ten years watching customs officials laugh at your hair?

- You're not taking this seriously at all, are you?

- Go away and come back when you're ready to do it properly.

- Unbelievable.

HENSGATE MULTI-MEDIA MEETING AREA

(Formerly Hensgate Public Library)

The centrepiece of Hensgate's £3-billion regeneration project opens November 2007.

The Hensgate Multi-Media Meeting Area boasts a multi-million-pound IT lab and a Pageturner's book store that allows customers to *BUY* their books rather than *BORROW* them. The centre also boasts:

- Disability Access
- 700-Space Car Park
- Pizza Town (restaurant)
- Zac's (wine bar and eatery)
- Gift Shop
- Tourist Information Office
- 36 VidiScreens
- Seasonal Ice-Skating Rink
- "Bungee-Jump" Trampolines
- Da Hang Out (games arcade and youth drop-in centre)
- Phone-Charging Sockets
- Ringtone Download Stations
- Orchid Night Club
- Communal Drumkit
- Primal Scream Therapy
- Advertising Hoardings

Registration for your voice-recognition, fingerprint sensitive AccessCard starts 23 November. Register in person at Site Office, Millennium Plain, Bank Street, Hensgate.

Hensgate *DISTRICT* Council
Re-branding Desperately

S = D/T Deliveries

We've travelled over seas, mountains and rivers (not to mention numerous municipal roads) to get your package to you on time and you didn't even have the decency to be in to sign for it.

You've got three options now:

A) Just forget all about it. It probably wasn't that important anyway.

B) Ring us on 0800 540976 to arrange a more convenient time, though I wouldn't hold your breath. We kind of feel that we've fulfilled our part of the bargain so we're likely to be unhelpful, surly and borderline aggressive.

C) Come and collect it from our pick-up depot (see instructions below).

Collection Instructions

Our depot is situated on the Isle of Doom, just off the western Scottish coast. Travel there can be treacherous, so we do advise enlisting the services of a local guide.

Directions: Head north on the M74. About fifteen miles before you reach Glasgow, turn off on to a craggy mountain pass. Follow the A71 for three days. At sunset on the third day, you'll see a hangman's tree and to the west, a barren wasteland populated by a desperate forgotten people. This is Kilmarnock. Follow a compass bearing of exactly 229 degrees, which will take you south-west, past the haunted Caves of Zargon and on to Royal Troon Golf Course, regular host of the British Open. Past Troon, you'll find a mysterious boatman, who will ferry you to our pick-up depot. Do not look him in the eye.

Please remember to bring the skin of a Nemean Lion, Hippolyte's belt and two forms of ID. And whilst you're here, if you wouldn't mind cleaning out the Stables of Augeas, that'd be great.

S = D/T Deliveries (UK Ltd), 4 Birley Road, London NE1 4AT

Hey You!

Having a lovely time, wish you were
here! Morocco is mad! Every time
you go out of the complex you get
hassled! The weather has been
absolutely gorgeous though. I've been
sitting by the pool all day doing sod
all! Kev's been off doing activities
and such like. He's been hanging
around with this local lad called
Hassan quite a lot. Bloody charming,
leaving me here on my tod! On our
HONEYMOON! I saw them holding
hands yesterday. Kev says that's
just their custom over here, but it
creeps me out a bit. Still, it's good
for him to unwind away from work.
Back home a week on Tuesday. Bye!

Sis!

p.s. Kev's a bit upset I mentioned
the holding hands thing. Don't tell
anyone. It's probably nothing.
See ya soon!!

SlowSlowLane.com

Over 50?
Got 15 years no claims?
Own a flat cap?

The good folk at SlowSlowLane.com **WILL** save you money on your car insurance. SlowSlowLane.com has been created **by** safe drivers **for** safe drivers who enjoy the pace of life in the slow lane.

In this 'compensation culture' riddled with political correctness, decent folk like you are left to pay the bill for those who can't be bothered to work, learn to do things in the correct manner, or look after things the proper, English way.

But there are some ways we can fight back!

If you're a slow driver, why should you have to pay higher insurance premiums because boy racers and immigrants can't drive properly? That's why, if you're over 50, have 15 years no claims and have parents who were born in this country, we guarantee to beat your car insurance renewal quote.

SlowSlowLane.com refuses to be regulated by the financial services authority. For full terms and conditions please go to www.slowslowlane.com/ourwayonthehighway.

Foreigners need not apply.

ETERNAL SUMMER

When you walk into an eternal summer tanning salon, you can be certain you'll get three things:

PROFESSIONALISM
GREAT VALUE FOR MONEY
A TAN

We use the very latest in ultra-violet treated polyhydrate compounds, microwave technology and state-of-the-art skin dyes to give you a healthy, bronzed appearance with minimal risk of permanent scarring, premature ageing or cancer. Our experienced skin technicians will install you in one of our world famous SunPods and answer any questions you might have before the procedure begins (subject to legal advice). We provide all the equipment you'll need for a happy and problem-free tanning experience – eye protectors, ergonomically designed limb restraints, even a complementary groin shield for added fertility.

The procedure itself is very simple, combining a controlled amount of dermal scorching with all the benefits of our specially formulated "skin-tar". This is then complemented by the careful application of high-frequency radiation, administered in short, intense bursts. You will then be given, completely free of charge, a set of full-body bandages and dressings in order to speed the healing process.

We do recommend that you try not to go outside, eat or sleep too heavily for at least seventy-two hours after the procedure. We know that keeping your bandages on all this time might seem like a pity – after all, you want to show off your new tan! However, it's worth remembering that, until you heal, you won't have a tan so much as a series of severe chemical burns regularly haemorrhaging pus.

This is an appeal on behalf of

Please recycle this leaflet.

Give someone the gift of giving

(by giving to someone else)

It can be so hard to know what to buy for someone you love. Whether it's their birthday, Christmas, an anniversary or the sacred feast day of Baal, you have to select a gift that not only meets with their approval, but says something about yourself. If you get it wrong, you could cause irreparable damage to your relationship. If that DVD isn't the special edition, if they've read that book before, if the puppy suffocated in the box, the celebrations are very definitely over. If only there was another option! If only there was a safe choice!

Now there is. Rather than hunting through bookshops and mail-order catalogues, why not reward someone with the gift of giving? For as little as £14/month, you could donate to charity on your loved one's behalf, providing disadvantaged people in some country somewhere (probably one of those ones with all the flies) with the essential resources they need. At a stroke, you sidestep the whole problem of choosing an appropriate gift; after all, who could possibly object to helping others less privileged and racked with middle-class guilt than themselves? Best of all, by taking the moral high ground, you avoid the ugly silence that follows the unwrapping of yet another gift voucher.

But that's not all! Now you can personalise your gift to suit the recipient. For a one-off payment of just £60, we'll give you a card with a picture of a goat and a printed assurance that your donation has gone directly towards buying a goat (or similar animal) for an African village. What they do with the goat (donkey/ostrich/marmot) once we've left is anybody's guess, but it's probably going to come in handy for something. Maybe they can charge tourists to go for rides on its back. Anyway, the point is, they'll have a goat. And you'll have a photo of a goat. With a lovely woolly goat face. It may not be the most practical gift, but who wants a card with a picture of a clean water supply? No one, that's who.

Of course, the money may not go entirely towards an actual goat. That would be ridiculous. There are various administrative costs to consider – staff wages, rent for our London headquarters, the cost of that tiny pen we send you every couple of months, postage for the goat, making sure the goat's passport is in order, getting the goat its jabs and everything – so it's hardly unreasonable to tell you that, of your £60 donation, only £6 will go towards buying the goat. By which point, let's be honest, it's hardly worth getting. Especially when there are lots of perfectly good animals that can be picked up on the cheap. We'll definitely send something, even if it's a cat from the alley behind our office.

Look, it's not our fault this doesn't really work. It wasn't us who got bored with donating to charity in a normal, practical way. If novelty is what it takes to get past your so-called "compassion fatigue", novelty's what you'll get, whether it makes sense or not. Just don't write to us in three months' time asking how the goat's doing, okay? You're the one who stopped us just sending food parcels. It's your bloody goat. You deal with it.

MONTAGUE STREET

"News & Views!"

Hi! And welcome to the first edition of the Montague Street Neighbourhood Watch newsletter! Don't worry, this isn't about "naming and shaming" anyone or saying who takes their bins in after the lorry's been and who leaves them out in the road for three days! This newsletter is just a way for us all to keep in touch and let everyone know what's going on. After all, we all live together, so why can't we have a bit of fun and keep our street safe at the same time! That's what the Neighbourhood Watch is all about: being good neighbours. And watching each other. Only kidding! On a serious note though, it is important in these worrying times of terrorist atrocities and Islamic fundamentalism for us all to remain vigilant for everyone's safety. Anyway, on with the newsletter!

NEWS

• As I'm sure you're all aware, the council has extended their "Keen to be Green" recycling zone out to our little corner of the world and it's up to all of us to put our boxes out every Tuesday with glass, cans and newspapers separated properly. I know it can seem like a bit of a pain, especially if you get through a good few bottles of wine a week (naming no names, Nigel Harrington!) but I don't have to remind you that climate change threatens the entire world, both economically and socially.

• I've had a meeting with Sergeant Foster from the local police station. Don't worry! He's not trying to arrest anyone on our road or give any of us an "asbo"! He just wanted to let us know that there have been some reports of youths outside the newsagents on Hall Road, so everyone needs to be extra vigilant for any joyriding, arson, gang violence and/or rape.

• As regards parking, there have been concerns among residents that some other residents are parking on the pavement when they have perfectly good driveways they could use. This causes a potential safety risk to pedestrians, especially as your house is directly opposite the busy turning on to Churchill Street.

• At the end of this month, we need to select one person to attend the Resident's Council Neighbourhood Seminar and report back to the rest of us. It was suggested that Sarah Harrington go, but as she's no longer technically a resident on this road, she wouldn't be able to liaise with the rest of us properly, unless she does it when she comes with the removal van next week.

VIEWS

This is the section of the newsletter where any resident who wants to get something off their chest or just start an interesting discussion can give the rest of us the benefit of their wisdom. As this is the first edition, I thought I'd kick things off with a short editorial on <u>BEING SUPPORTIVE</u>.

In these troubled times of war, financial uncertainty, hoodies and abortion, it's important that we have someone to turn to when everything goes wrong. For me, that's God, but I know not everyone shares my strong, life-affirming faith. So where can those without God turn in a time of need? Well, the answer's right in front of you: each other. I know it's not a very "trendy" word these days, but I'm a firm believer in <u>community</u> and <u>neighbourliness</u>. If we share the burden between all of us, our particular load won't seem quite so impossibly, crushingly heavy.

We live in a changing world. Nowadays, there's no such thing as a job for life and unemployment is something that can happen to any one of us at any time, unless we've already retired with a secure and well-structured pension plan. Another thing that doesn't last for ever any more is marriage. A huge number of modern marriages end in divorce and it's really nothing to be ashamed of, even if you are too old to start "dating" again and will probably not find another partner. Likewise, a lot of people don't see depression as a real "disease", but it is. It's a "disease" just as real as flu or AIDs, and it should be treated as such. It's a serious concern for all of us, in theory, but more so for those who have less to live for. It can strike at any time, like a killer virus or disability. Depression is a very real and serious problem and there's actual medical proof for it being some kind of scientific fact, even if, to an outsider, it just looks like lazing around in your dressing gown all day and not bothering to shave.

Don't worry, though! It might be a disease, but it isn't contagious, or certainly not over the course of a five-minute chat! With that in mind, all of us can afford to take some time to <u>be supportive</u> and be <u>good neighbours</u> to each other. If we can rely on each other, we can make it through, pull ourselves together and start mowing the lawn properly again. So <u>lend a hand</u>, or a <u>friendly ear</u>. Everybody needs <u>understanding friends</u> from time to time and it doesn't hurt to <u>pop round</u> once in a while for a quick <u>chat</u>.

And if you can't manage that, at least give Nigel a hand bringing the bins in, because there's nothing more likely to aggravate clinical depression than knowing that you're being a burden on your neighbours and cluttering up the pavement.

BYE!

Well, that's all for this month! Thanks for reading and I'm sure I'll bump into each of you in the next few days and we can catch up then (those of you who still leave the house, that is!).

Remember, our Neighbourhood Watch Scheme is there for all of us, so don't be afraid to come to me with any concerns you might have about unsafe window boxes, "chav" boy racers or the Asian family who've just moved into number 23. I haven't sent them a copy of this newsletter because I'm not sure how well they speak English, but if you do manage to talk to them, welcome them to the area and try and find out exactly how Muslim they are, because I'm not sure what those red headscarves mean.

Till next time then! Bye!!!

Cooking Instructions

Oven: Pre-heat oven to gas mark 7, 220°C for an electric oven, 200°C for a fan-assisted or, if you have an Aga, just hot enough to melt a pair of dark green galoshes. Place directly on to oven shelf, shoo the dogs away (they can be such a bother), allow to cook for precisely one episode of *The Archers* and serve with a really rather lovely Pinot Noir you brought back from Sicily last year.

Microwave: Clear the work surface of screaming illegitimate children and piles of unpaid mobile bills before opening packaging. Hack at film lid with whatever comes to hand and place in filth-encrusted microwave for 3 minutes at full whack. This will give you time to smoke half a Mayfair and save the other half for later. Serve with supermarket own-brand lager and primetime ITV.

Lifetime Guarantee –
La Faute Cookware – Frying Pan

All La Faute cookware comes with
a lifetime guarantee, so you can rest
assured that you will never need to
purchase another frying pan for the
entire lifetime of this frying pan.

From Then To Now:
An Interview With Uta Reinseiger

Simply the way he walks into a room, the way he holds himself and the weight of his steps across the smooth walnut floor is enough to remind you of the man he once was, the man he still, in many significant and intangible ways, subtly yet all but overwhelmingly, in the (it is barely the right word yet unmistakably the correct one to use) twilight of his life, is. He places two long, slender glasses of water on the table between us and I cannot help but notice the self-contained assurance of his movements, their intricate ballet of memory, enlightenment and – could it be, I ask myself before instantly coming to the realisation that I already know the answer – regret. He carries with him the weight, both metaphorical and literal, of his years.

"Mr Reinseiger will be with you shortly," he says. I nod and watch the play of the cool, clear (indeed, transparent) water in the delicately polished vessels before me. They bend, strain and refract the light that passes through them, creating illusions as potent as those of a veteran magician. Indeed, refraction is perhaps an apposite metaphor

for the complex series of events that has brought Uta Reinseiger to where he is today, a pertinent simile for the manifold twists and turns in the life of this fascinating, compelling man as he has journeyed through a cruel, kind and ultimately unpredictable world – a journey, one might say, from then to now.

His arrival occurs exactly as I imagined it would – with him walking across the floor of the restaurant and sitting in the chair opposite me. It is hard to convey exactly how it feels to be in the presence of a man who is, by all accounts, as much as the phrase can be considered to be appropriate in this, or, indeed, any, scenario, inasmuch as anyone could be described as such, a truly great man. What to say? How to behave? These are questions.

"Hello," he says.

And there it is – straightforward, brusque yet charming, subtly workman-like, strangely vulnerable and deceptive in its simplicity. How representative of his character this greeting is. Like Reinseiger himself, it is unadorned yet enigmatic. The way his voice rises from silence, the subtle breath of the first letter blossoming into, before one expects it, a fully formed syllable; the way the word seems to rotate on its axis like a planet as the delicate trill of that double L becomes a fulcrum for the entire statement; the way the final vowel is formed, strong and resilient, before fading and eventually dissipating like mist rising from the surface of a heated swimming pool on a cold autumn night – these nuances of idiosyncratic perspicacity leave me, as they would leave any listener, humbled by the quiet dignity and unmistakable humanity of a life at its very literal perihelion.

Suddenly, I am acutely aware of the gulf between us: he is a legend, a living myth, a monument to greatness built in flesh and warm, vital breath; while I – I am nothing; an ant beside a colossus, a worm beneath a palace, a fruit fly in the shadow of the pyramids. What can I possibly say that would be worthy of the attention of such a man? He is, as no reasonable person could possibly doubt, the greatest thinker of our time. His concerns are not the concerns of the thronging populace, his thoughts not our thoughts, his feelings not our feelings. What does it matter to him that we, we who are so unquestionably his inferiors, suffer and toil? We are as dust to him. Does a man concern himself with the suffering of dust? Does he stop to worry about the dust's health, or the dust's financial situation? Does he ever pause to consider that the dust may have made the biggest mistake of its life and may only just be realising it, years later? Does he have any idea that the dust sometimes cries itself to sleep with a bottle of cheap Rioja and reams of internet pornography? No, he does not.

I summon all my faculties and begin.

[CONTINUED ON PAGES 7, 8, 9, 13, 14, 26–32, 41 & BACK COVER]

TV Listings

NEWS24

05:00	News
06:00	News
07:00	News
08:00	News
08:30	Breakfast News
08:45	News
08:52	News
09:00	News
10:00	News
11:00	News
12:00	Lunchtime News
13:00	News
14:00	News
15:00	News
16:00	News
16:24	Tea & Biscuits News
17:00	News
17:30	News
18:00	News
18:30	News
19:00	Dinner News
20:00	News
21:00	News
22:00	News
23:00	Feeling A Bit Peckish Before Bedtime News
00:00	News
01:00	News
02:00	News
03:00	News
04:00	News

SITCOM CENTRAL

05:00	Dougie, Howard & Beth
05:30	Dougie, Howard & Beth
06:00	Dougie, Howard & Beth
06:30	Don't Go There
07:00	Upside Town
07:30	Dougie, Howard & Beth
08:00	Five Kids And A Dog Called Jack
08:30	Five Kids And A Dog Called Jack
09:00	Capital Punishment
09:30	Capital Punishment
10:00	Rodeo Dad
10:30	Dougie, Howard & Beth
11:00	Rodeo Dad
11:30	Don't Go There
12:00	Rodeo Dad
12:30	Upside Town
13:00	Four Kids And A Dog Called Jack
13:30	Don't Go There
14:00	Don't Go There
14:30	Don't Go There
15:00	Don't Go There
15:30	Don't Go There
16:00	Don't Go There
16:30	Don't Go There
17:00	Capital Punishment
17:30	Don't Go There
18:00	Don't Go There
18:30	Don't Go There

19:00 Dougie, Howard & Beth
All hell breaks loose when Beth finds a family of illegal immigrants living in her garage and Dougie gets a new job at the Homeland Security Department. (R) (S) 3073-5466-112

19:30 Capital Punishment
There's a new face on death row when Frank's lawyer lets him down. Unfortunately, as love-struck Jimmy is about to find out, Frank isn't the only one who's lost his appeal. (R) (S) 8492-8726-320

20:00 Dougie, Howard & Beth
Howard is having trouble adjusting to his new gender, while Beth and Dougie have been misdiagnosed with each other's cancers after a mix-up at the hospital. (R) (S) 0065-5466-002

20:30 Don't Go There
In an act of cruel and premeditated brutality, Latisha forces Chantelle to "talk to the hand". There's also a tedious subplot involving a lost cat. (R) (S) 5444-9007-656

21:00 Dougie, Howard & Beth
The gang are caught up in a tense hostage situation and for some reason, Dougie is suffering from uncontrollable flatulence. The whole thing smacks of lazy writing. (R) (S) 2047-5466-812

21:30 Rodeo Dad
After 136 episodes, Mikey has finally begun to suspect that his father is in fact a professional rodeo clown in this unfunny and ill-thought-through sitcom. (R) (S) 2210-8654-000

22:00 Don't Go There
Oh God, this one again. Well, the plot is pretty much the same every time, so my summary becomes superfluous if you've ever had the misfortune to see an episode. (R) (S) 2020-9007-941

22:30 Upside Town
I mean, have you actually watched these things? Have you ever actually sat down and watched them? Week after week, episode after episode. It's just relentless. (R) (S) 8005-7403-997

23:00 Dougie, Howard & Beth
A misunderstanding takes place. One character is hilariously camp and makes innuendos. Someone repeats someone else but changes the word order slightly. There must be more to life than this. (R) (S) 1111-5466-067

23:30 Capital Punishment
I mean, what's it all for? What's it actually for, this stuff? What is it supposed to do? I can't remember the last time I laughed. I mean, a real, honest belly-laugh that makes you feel that everything might just be all right after all. What happened to them? I'm sure I used to laugh. (R) (S) 6300-8726-771

00:00 Dougie, Howard & Beth
Is it only me, or does everyone feel like this? When did we stop laughing? When did "comedy" become a genre instead of a device and lose all its power? These things aren't comedy. They aren't funny. They don't make life better. (R) (S) 1010-5466-333

00:30 Rodeo Dad
Mikey spooks the horses whilst rehearsing for the big talent show. Steve loses his hat. Miranda discovers she is pregnant. But who's the father? (R) (S) 8349-8654-150

01:00 Don't Go There
01:30 Three Kids And A Dog Called Jack
02:00 Capital Punishment
02:30 Two Kids And A Dog Called Jack
03:00 Dougie, Howard & Beth
03:30 Don't Go There
04:00 Dougie, Howard & Beth
04:30 Two Kids And The Tattered Remains Of A Collar

TONIGHT'S TV PICKS

Five Children & I.T. – 9 p.m., Channel 4
Dismal modernisation of Nesbitt's children's classic. Five East London teenagers find a Samsung mobile phone in a back alley. They try to text "bo & ting" to another friend, but instead of sending the message the phone begins to talk to them and offers them a wish each. The next 55 minutes are taken up with the director's own right-wing assertions that all people wish for in life is a sturdy house in the suburbs and a good burglar alarm. Avoid. **JB**

The 4th Emergency Service – 8 p.m., BBC1
A special hour-long episode with Birmingham's finest breakdown service men and women. Pete is still trying to come to terms with Lil's death, while Suze and Ross have a suspicious call from the owner of a Toyota Prius – "More likely to be the electrics than the engine," Suze says. Meanwhile, back at base, the Harvest Festival party kicks off with karaoke that shatters the myth that all AA representatives can sing. **JB**

Radio 4 on BBC1 – 10 p.m., BBC1
Not really a pick, but this is notable as being indicative of the deep, deep trouble the BBC is in. Radio 4 on BBC1 is, as the title suggests, whatever happens to be on Radio 4 at the time (in this case From Our Own Woman's Island) being played over a child's crayon drawing of the BBC Director General being hung. We'll talk about this in years to come. **JB**

Side Order's Red Sauce
serving suggestions

Side Order's Red Sauce is designed as a delicious accompaniment to any dish. Why not splash a little on that boring old spud? How about adding a little colour to that carbonara? And with **Side Order's Red Sauce**, who said salad has to be completely tasteless? You can even use it as a funky kind of red butter if you want.

This week's taste-tastic recipe:
Crimson Houmous

Simply take 100g of normal full-fat houmous, mix in 12 tablespoons of **Side Order's Red Sauce** and serve with savoury biscuits. Yum!

NB
Side Order's Red Sauce is intended as a delicious accompaniment to a main dish. Side Order's Red Sauce should not be eaten on its own. It is NOT a substitute for a meal. KJH Chemicals will not be held responsible for the death of customers who persist in eating this stuff day in, day out without consuming anything else. It's preposterous that we should even be 'legally and morally bound' to add this warning; it's clearly not a suitable foodstuff for exclusive consumption. Why anyone would want to live on it even after it became apparent that it was killing them is beyond us. Just because we recently suggested eating it with a delicate Béarnaise sauce and we're patently not concerned with the fripperies of so-called 'healthy eating' doesn't mean we want people to die. For Christ's sake, why not try pointing the finger of blame at the public once in a while? Corporations are busting their asses (if you'll excuse the phrase!) to get people to like them. We make products that people like. We pour millions of dollars into research and development just to make sure that we're always bringing out great products and all everyone ever says is, "Oh, look at Side Order, they're just like a big crack-dealer for fat kids." Yes, there's a lot of sugar in our products, but that's because you all want sugar, right up until the moment someone dies and then you all pretend you can't stand the stuff. We just can't win. So we've made a resolution. We're going to keep on producing stuff you like and stuff you buy, we're going to keep on making our money (hey, we have an OBLIGATION to our shareholders) and when you get all worked up and start saying mean things, we're just not going to listen. Sound fair? Of course it doesn't, but we're just going to rise above it and be the bigger man. And you can do your exposés, you can publish your editorials, you can launch your multi-billion-dollar law suits, we're just not going to listen. Okay?

Bottled at source by KJH Chemicals – a family multinational corporation. KJH House // Tiller's Road // Uxbridge. UX90 7GH

WE ❤ MOTORS

Renault Clio 1.4v (1998) Red. Enjoys weekends away, MSAs and Ikea carparks. Looking for companionship. Must have GSOH & full UK driving licence. £2,378

Ford Escort 1.6 (1997) Crimson. I want someone who'll drive me hard and fast, take me to the drive-through and not worry about my slack gearbox. I'm cheap! £650 ono

BMW 5 Series (2000) Black. Fittie wanted for commutes, nights out and speeding. Must be under 30, with good job and highlights. £7,000

Volvo S40 (2005) Metallic Grey. Look, I'm jolly cross about even being in here; I'm brand new, there's nothing wrong with me. I'm safe, reliable and I'd say pretty damn aspirational, but apparently not as aspirational as a Saab. £12,450

Rover 200 2.4 (1992) Brown. Widower who takes life at gentle pace. Enjoys trips to the seaside, Classic FM and country drives. Looking for long-lasting friendship. Over 50s only. £1,900

Citroen 2CV (1996) Yellow. Do you like foreign cinema, bubble baths & driving in circles? I'm weird, wacky and wonderful. I'm not everyone's cup of tea but you might like me. £900 ono

Lotus Elise 111R (2005) Yellow. It breaks his heart. It breaks mine, but life's a bitch and then you marry one. He didn't make her send the kids back and get a huge great fuck-off Japanese replacement, did he? My god, I'm so, so beautiful. £22,975

MAURICE VANNS

THE NAKED PRESIDENTS (VOL. 1)

"Even the President of the United States
sometimes must stand naked."
Bob Dylan

It was one of Dylan's most enduring lyrics. A line that bored deep into the hearts of corporate and political America, a refrain heard (probably) above the noise at anti-war rallies in the sixties, a vision that remains as potent today as it did back then. The President himself stood there in the minds of his people stark naked. Powerful is an understatement.

Now, some four decades later, Dylan's original vision has been realised by one of the UK's most unique and exciting musical talents: Maurice Vanns. **The Naked Presidents (Vol. 1)** features twelve original songs, each dedicated to describing with breathtaking literalness the naked form of a different American President. From Abraham Lincoln's elbow to the buttocks of John Quincy Adams, **The Naked Presidents (Vol. 1)** is nothing if not thorough.

It is a testament to Vanns' enduring talent that no two Presidents sound the same naked; from the delicate finger-picked ballad 'Thomas Jefferson (nude)' to the rockabilly closer 'I Can See Your Pubes, Zachary Taylor', this plethora of experimental sonorous tracts is flawlessly stitched together by Vanns's rich semi-baritone musings.

With **The Naked Presidents (Vol. 1)**, Vanns finally proves the little-heard maxim 'With nakedness comes poignancy.' I hope you enjoy this album as much as I enjoyed making it.

Maurice Vanns, Cambridge, UK

TRACK LISTING

1. Elbows and All (George Washington)/VANNS - 3.56
2. John Adams's Apple/VANNS - 1.41
3. Thomas Jefferson (nude)/VANNS - 12.03
4. Madison's Square Garden (of strawberry-blonde pubic hair)/VANNS - 4.15
5. James Monroe's Nose/VANNS - 3.45
6. I Wish I Was You, John Quincy Adams/VANNS - 0.30
7. How He Strides (Andrew Jackson)/VANNS - 3.34
8. Six Inch Shins (Martin Van Buren)/VANNS - 4.57
9. Willy's Willy (William Henry Harrison)/VANNS - 16.23
10. John (John Tyler)/VANNS - 2.38
11. James! Knox! Polk!/VANNS - 1.49
12. I Can See Your Pubes, Zachary Taylor/VANNS - 4.02

All tracks recorded. Many thanks to my ex-wife Suzanne, my dog Butler and, of course, all those naked dead men in my head.

There is no 'friendship'.

There is no 'understanding'.

There is no 'love'.

There's just ...

THE HUNT

The Hunt is more than just a dating manual – it's a philosophy for life. Sure, it tells you how to pick up any girl you want. Yeah, it teaches you how to rule a room using just the subtleties of body language. And of course, it shows you how to be in control of any situation, anywhere. But there's so much more ...

'*The Hunt* is a shockingly . . . astounding . . . read.'
PLATFORM

'Breathtakingly dangerous. I kept trying to put it down
but a kind of horrified fascination at its sheer unabashed
. . . really . . . good . . . ness . . . kept stopping me short.'
THE SENTINEL

'All you ever wanted to know about sex
but wished you hadn't asked.'
THE NEWS

ISBN 978-0-141-03168-2

9 780141 031682

THE HUNT   CHAPTER 4

Killing The 'F' Word

Do you know what the worst word in the English language is? Here's a clue: it begins with 'F'. That's right, I'm talking about the word 'friend'. As a player, you should learn to hate the word 'friend', because, along with syphilis and feminism, it's your worst enemy. Just picture it: you and your target are sharing a drink, you've just used a Wallbreaker such as the ferret joke (see Chapter 3), you've reached Intimacy Stage 6, and then it happens. 'You're such a good friend.' Disaster! This is the worst possible thing you can hear. With that one terrible word, you're all the way back to Stage 2 and all your hard work has been for nothing.

So what do we do? Like they said in Scouts: be prepared. You've got to stop the 'F' word before it even happens – if she says it, it's already too late. You've got to stay one move ahead at all times. Remember, seduction is like a game of chess, except with sex at the end. And with less pieces on the board – just you and her. You've got to look like you're the knight when you're actually the king, and make her feel like the queen when she's actually a pawn. But if that pawn reaches the other side of the relationship board, it'll turn into a queen, so be careful.

Here are a few lines you can drop into conversation to stop the 'F' word before it even starts. Learn them and use them whenever you can:

'Don't you agree that people only say they're your friend if they want something? We both know that's how it works.'

'I could never be friends with someone like you. We're just too different – I'm charismatic, witty and incredible in bed while you're intelligent, beautiful and sexy. It'd never work. Not as a friendship. No.'

'Friendship is bullshit, everyone knows that. You'd have to be so naïve to think that anyone was actually your friend. [LAUGH] Naïve and sexy.'

'God, I hate you so much. Will you sleep with me?'

```
dno м8 lt м no
wn uv fnd pb мt
cм :-/ 18rz
```

Stick riot down
the sub rounds
home, but I night
hive it a nips and
ruby in. Poppy.
Quill can't york
this ducking
shone. Duck it!

THESE PREMISES ARE LICENSED FOR THE SALE OF INTOXICATING LIQUOR, CHEESE TOASTIES AND ILL-INFORMED OPINIONS ON THE CORRECT MANAGEMENT OF FOOTBALL CLUBS COMPETING AT AN INTERNATIONAL LEVEL.

IMAGINAIRE ENFANT®
"Ce slogan est en Français"

PRESENTING IMAGINAIRE ENFANT® – THE NEW LOW-ALCOHOL LAGER FROM IMAGINAIRE – FRANCE'S MOST KEENLY EXPORTED LAGER. IMAGINAIRE ENFANT® IS A MODERN BEER FOR THE MODERN DRINKER. WITH ONLY 2% ALCOHOL CONTENT, YOU CAN ENJOY THE ACRID GASSY TASTE OF LAGER ALL EVENING AND STILL WAKE UP AS FRESH AS A DAISY.

GOT A BIG MEETING IN THE MORNING AND AREN'T PREPARED TO BE SEEN DRINKING LEMONADE? WANT YOUR WIFE TO LET YOU HOLD YOUR CHILD AGAIN, BUT REFUSE TO GIVE UP THE COMFORT OF YOUR EIGHT PINTS A NIGHT? LOVE DRINKING *AND* DRIVING?

Sorry, just
read that back
and realised it
was complete
bollocks. What I
meant to say was
no, I probably
won't be coming
out tonight. But
have one for me.
Cheerio.

Ye Olde Englishe

Really Real

Crisps

~ Since 2006 ~

WILD SWAN & PINE NEEDLE

We hope you enjoy the curious and delectable taste of Ye Olde Englishe Really Real Crisps. We think you'll find them more real than your average potato snack. Our hand-picked King Edward potatoes are nothing if not authentic. Aged three, they are abandoned in a Victorian orphanage. Here they reside until they are eight, when they are turned out on the cold streets of London's East End, where they embark on a life of petty crime and musical theatre. After a brief stay in Newgate Gaol for public indecency, they are chopped into thick(ish) slices, sprinkled with sumptuous Wild Swan and Pine Needle 'flavouring dust' and bagged up in an authentic Ye Olde Englishe Really Real Crisp bag.

Ingredients:
Raw uncooked potato, flavouring.

Other Flavours:
Marinated Gristle and Fractured Pink Peppercorns

Wild Boar and Rhubarb

Ye Olde Real Derbyshire Blue Stilton with Normandy Infant Shallots Pickled in a Crisp 2004 Chardonnay Cherry Vinegar

Ready Salted

MANGO DASH @ MYRIAD @ METROPOLIS @ EDGE @ THE PYTHON ROOMS @ SNAIL @ F>E>L>I>X>

SEVEN FLOORS OF BONK-CORE BELLYBEATS AND SCREWBALL MASH-UP MADNESS. GOT THE WINTER BLUES? BOSH 'EM HERE!

MAIN ARENA: DJ FUKWIT / ROGET & THE THESPS / MC STALIN'S REVENGE CHILL OUT ARENA: ICE, WATER & PARAMEDICS

10–10.30 P.M. @ F>E>L>I>X> / TCR / LUNDUN TAAN ENTRY: £15 OR £20 WITH FLYER

HOGALICIOUS®
PORK SCRATCHINGS

We scratch only the finest Wessex Saddlebacks to create the unique taste extravaganza of Hogalicious®. We then coat the scratchings in hand-picked Atlantic sea salt and lusty aromatic spices before lovingly burning them in our specially designed kiln ovens. Lice and ticks are gently encouraged away from the scratchings as they mature in our warehouses for anything up to a fortnight. Finally, the scratchings are vacuum-sealed in our state-of-the-art packaging shed and rushed to you in vans made from only the purest fibreglass and aluminium.

INGREDIENTS:

Salt (80%), Pepper, Thyme, Onion, Grit, Pig (trace)

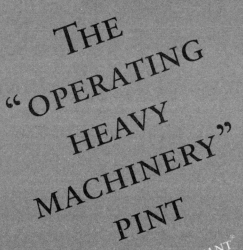

THE "OPERATING HEAVY MACHINERY" PINT

IMAGINAIRE ENFANT®
"Ce slogan est en Français"

Soz buddy. Already
out & about on
town. Not sure
where going next.
Crazy! Have a gr8
eve! Xxx ps have
you tried Darren?

The
"I'm a
Recovering
Alcoholic"
Pint

Imaginaire Enfant®
"Ce slogan est en Français"

OH, INCIDENTALLY THERE'S A RUMOUR GOING ROUND THAT THERE MIGHT BE A BIT OF DISCOTHÈQUE HAPPENING, AT SOME POINT ...

· ·

unsigned / three-piece / orchestral / grunge / punk / metal / hip hop / lo-fi / urban / thrash / house / garage / lounge / kitchen / two-up two-down / ambient / euphoric / chill-out / balearic / funk / skiffle-rock / indie pop band from just outside of Chichester

· ·

We're all in the gutter but some of us are at

OH, INCIDENTALLY THERE'S A RUMOUR GOING ROUND THAT THERE MIGHT BE A BIT OF DISCOTHÈQUE HAPPENING, AT SOME POINT ...

Sam's House / 93 Stepney Road / Hackney / E9 / Bring a bottle

CLEAR: Hello
customer. If you've
been on the same
contract for more
than a year, you
may be eligible for
a handset upgrade.
To find out, visit
our website at
www.clearmeout.
com and click on
"Orientation Film".
Close the curtains
and look directly
into the screen.
Tell no one what
you saw.

Hey wasss-up!!
Nah, I'm @ home
saving it up for
nite out w lucy
allcock - u up 4
that? daz

THE
" IN COURT
TOMORROW
MORNING "
PINT

IMAGINAIRE ENFANT®
"Ce slogan est en Français"

THIS IS A RESIDENTIAL AREA. PLEASE
RESPECT OUR NEIGHBOURS BY LEAVING
QUIETLY. OR, FAILING THAT, BY NOT
BEING SICK IN THEIR FLOWERBEDS. AND
NOT HAVING DRUNKEN FIGHTS WHICH
CAREEN, OUT OF CONTROL, INTO THEIR
GREENHOUSES. IT'S NOT EVEN REALLY
AN ISSUE OF RESPECT; IT'S JUST COMMON
COURTESY NOT TO URINATE THROUGH
SOMEONE'S LETTERBOX. AFTER ALL, WE
LIVE IN A SOCIETY, AND SOCIETIES WORK
ON THE BASIS OF MUTUALLY AGREED
STANDARDS OF BEHAVIOUR WHICH
NORMALLY (EXCEPTING SOME CORNISH
TRADITIONS) PRECLUDE THE ACT OF
RELIEVING ONESELF THROUGH A HOLE
IN SOMEONE ELSE'S FRONT DOOR. SORRY,
THIS IS COMING OFF SOUNDING HEAVIER
THAN I'D INTENDED. LOOK, I'M NOT
TRYING TO DENY YOU YOUR FREE WILL
OR ANYTHING, I'M JUST SAYING DON'T
PISS EVERYWHERE, ALL RIGHT? THAT'S
ALL. AND DON'T TAKE YOUR TROUSERS
OFF AND SIT IN THE MIDDLE OF THE
ROAD SINGING THE CHORUS TO ROBBIE
WILLIAMS' "ANGELS" OVER AND OVER
AGAIN. THAT'S NOT OKAY.

S = D/T Deliveries

We called AGAIN and you weren't in. AGAIN.

We're sorry that it had to come to this.

We ARe holding yOUR PACkAGe hoStAge. We WANt twO FORMS OF PhOTO Id. LeAVe The Id IN A BLACk BAG MARked 'SWAG' IN The Old ABANdONed WARehOUSe NR. The heNSGATe INdUSTRIAL eSTATe. COMe ALONe. NO POLICe OR ROYAl MAIL.

S = D/T Deliveries (UK Ltd), 4 Birley Road, London NE1 4AT

THIS BIN BAG IS THE PROPERTY OF
HENSGATE DISTRICT COUNCIL.

THERE IS A £200 EXCESS ON ANY
DAMAGE CAUSED TO THE BAG IF YOU
ARE DEEMED TO BE RESPONSIBLE.

PARISHIONERS UNDER 25 MAY
HAVE TO PAY A SUPPLEMENT.

PLEASE DECLARE ANY PREVIOUS
MISDEMEANOURS RELATING
TO WASTE DISPOSAL.

DO NOT USE FOR ANYTHING
OTHER THAN RUBBISH.

FOR A DEFINITION OF 'RUBBISH' PLEASE GO
TO WWW.HENSGATE.GOV.UK/RUBBISH

COMPLETE OUR HOUSEHOLD WASTE SURVEY
FOR THE CHANCE TO WIN A FREE MP3 PLAYER.

Hensgate *DISTRICT* Council
Re-branding Desperately

❧GLOBETROTTER☙ ™

Globetrotter™ Old Irish Triple-Distilled Oak Cask All-American Sour Mash Whisky is distilled three times to give it the unmistakable flavor that only triple-distillation can create. It is then aged in oak casks made of no less than 80% Californian Oak and filtered through the finest charcoal, pewter and civet for that centuries-old traditional taste that has fascinated and provoked connoisseurs since the time of dawn.

In 1873, Josiah P. Hedenhöff left Ireland, where generations of his ancestors had been living for literally years, and set out to make a new life in America. It was a far from easy journey and his wife and two of his sons died on the crossing. But Josiah was undeterred and as soon as he arrived in Minnesota, he set about building a distillery. Before this could be completed, however, it collapsed, killing three of his sons and ruining his business. What Josiah needed was a miracle and, this being America, a miracle was what he got. Josiah's eldest son Zeke was panning for gold when he was attacked by a bear and killed. When Josiah followed the trail of torn innards into the hills, he found a cave where a hidden spring poured forth the purest mountain water. Within the year, he had built a new distillery on that very site. After this also collapsed, claiming the lives of four more of his sons and his second wife, he moved to Colorado and bought four low-rent industrial units under an assumed name before declaring himself bankrupt and faking his own death. This proved to be the miracle he had been looking for and it is here, in Enterprise Parks Colorado, that Globetrotter™ is made to this day, just in the way that Ol' Grandpappy Josiah™ would have wanted.

Please drink this entire bottle of Globetrotter™ responsibly.
Your statutory rights are not important.

Thank you for
contacting
ANSATXT. The
answer to your
question will
follow shortly.
There is a
charge of £2/
question. For
more information,
visit www.
ansatxt.co.uk.

ANSATXT:
Recognised cures
include egg
yolks mixed with
tomato juice and
Tabasco, strong
black coffee or
sports energy
drinks. However,
you could try
drinking a pint
of water before
you go to bed.

Welcome to The Kate Blackwell Fansite!

Kate Blackwell is one of the fittest girls to hit our screens in years. Most of you will know her from the TV series Diddlebury Close where she plays the excitable and lovely Jodie, but she's had bit parts in The Bill and EastEnders and has done loads of acting on stage. I will try and keep this site updated as regularly as possible, but if you hear of any Kate news do e-mail: <u>cliveb@BLTonline.org</u>

See ya!
Clive, September 2004

<u>KATE NEWS</u>
<u>BIOGRAPHY</u>
<u>FOTO GALLERY</u>
<u>FORUM</u>
<u>LINKS</u>
<u>ABOUT ME</u>

News Flashes

03-03-2006 – Sorry I haven't posted for a while.

04-01-2006 – Happy New Year

25-12-2006 – Happy Xmas! ☺

08-11-2005 – Look sorry I haven't posted for a while, but this is getting really stressful. It takes ages for my computer to load up and then the website making program keeps crashing. No one bothers posting on the forum anyway. It's really hard for me in Holme Firth to get to hear about all the stuff going on in 'trendy' London. I'm not even sure I like Kate as a person (although she's still well fit). I've written to her agent loads to tell her about this site and I've got nothing back off her at all. Sometimes I just wonder why I bother. It's loads of work you know, just thinking about it is really stressful.

20-09-2005 – The Kate Blackwell fansite is one year old!!

23-06-2005 – It's my birthday! ☺ Sorry I haven't posted for a while.

15-03-2005 – New Pic added

01-01-2005 – Happy New Year everyone!! ☺

25-12-2005 – Happy Christmas everyone!!!!!!! ☺☺☺

27-11-2004 – Sorry I haven't posted any news for a while. I've been trying to find out news on Kate. No news at present.

29-09-2004 – Panic over, <u>The Mirror</u> (click to read article – I think the link should be working) says Kate is staying, in fact she's been given a three year contract!!!!!!! ☺☺☺☺☺☺☺☺☺

24-09-2004 – I've heard rumours that Kate is leaving Diddlesbury Close!!!!!!!!!!!!!!!?????????? Can anyone confirm??????!!!!!!

21-09-2004 – Kate spotted coming out of Japanio Red in London's Soho with actor boyfriend (bastard! ;-)) Jeremy Ascott (Jimmy from Soloman's Wake). Thanks to Kate fan (and my sister!) Marianne for that one!

20-09-2004 – The world's first unofficial Kate Blackwell site is launched. Webmaster Clive Bennett said "this is a landmark day for fans of Kate. Why not join our forum! And remember keep those spotted's coming in!"

ABOUT ME

My name is Clive Bennett, though sometimes my friends call me "Gordon Bennett" because I can be a bit of a handful. I'm 43 years old and I live at home with my mum and three dogs – Benny, Stephen, and Xena. I know, I know, I still live with my mum, but I'm sure I'll meet the right girl one day!!!! ☺☺

I love Kate Blackwell from Diddlesbury Close. I think she's one of the best actresses to hit the TV screens in recent years. ☺ I think Kate's the kind of girl I'd like to marry one day. ☺☺ If you look like her, e-mail me!! cliveb@BLTonline.org.

I also love: Films, Soaps, chatting to my friends on MSN, doing pictures, and Kate Blackwell (had to mention that again!)

BACK

Welcome to the Kate Blackwell FORUM!!!!

Hello and welcome to the Kate Blackwell Forum. Please only discuss Kate Blackwell!!

20-09-2004 WEBMASTER Hi Everyone. Start Posting from Today

- No Replies

THE HUNT   CHAPTER 12

Endgame

By this point in the course, if you've been following the rules, you should be knee-deep in talent. Your black book (Book A) should be full of 9s and 10s, your brown book (Book B) should have a selection of 6s, 7s and 8s for use as diversions and foils and your red book (Book X) should be bulging with people you must spend the rest of your life avoiding. You might think that you've got it made, right? After all, this is the good life. This is what we set out to achieve. Think again, friend. See, this is just the beginning. This is where the hard work really starts.

For the average helpless schmo (AHS), it might seem like an impossible dream to have an endless string of 9s and 10s at his beck and call, but we know better. Using the techniques in the last eleven chapters, you now have the power to break any woman and bend her to your will (hey, she's yours now – bend her any way you like). But what happens when you want to move her from Book A to Book X? The longer you're in the game, the more hollow shells of once-proud women you'll have littering the path behind you. Sure, you could just walk away. You could X them whenever you want – that's the power you've earned. But used-up women are like nuclear waste. If you don't dispose of them in the right way, they can destroy you. They can make you sick. They can poison the ground you walk on and make it so nothing grows there ever again. So you're going to need an exit strategy.

There are two qualities that go to make up a good endgame: speed and finality. If you can balance these two criteria, you'll be saying goodbye for very definitely the last time. Speed is absolutely essential – you need to get out of there before she's even considered the possibility that you might want to. The longer you stay, the longer she has to try and work her emotional meathooks into you. You'll start to hear a lot of stuff about 'trust' and 'feelings' and, if she's really dangerous, 'love', but you've got to stop up your ears. You've got to tie yourself to the mast. Remember, love is something invented by women to keep men under control. You don't want to be under control. This is your game now. You've taken back the power. So when you walk away, make it final. Leave her in no doubt as to what's just happened. You wanted her, you took her and now you're finished. At this stage (and this is the only time I'll ever tell you this), be honest. Let her know that what's just happened, what you've just done to her, was a game. It was all a game and you've just won it. And as you walk off into the night, leaving her sitting with her heart jammed in her throat, wondering what happened, you'll start to feel that old familiar emptiness gathering in the base of your stomach. You are alone and complete and inviolable. You don't need any of them. You don't need anything. You are strong in your solitude. You are perfect. And that slow, empty nausea you feel – that is your soul.

ANSATXT: Traditional
remedies include
counting sheep or
reading. Try to
relax your entire
body. You may find
that breathing
exercises help.

ANSATXT: As well
as Job Centres,
there are many
recruitment
agencies and job-
search websites.
Before you start
searching,
consider carefully
what it is that
you want from a
job. This will
help you to find
something that's
right for you.

ANSATXT: Many
people find
that some form
of creative
activity gives
them an emotional
outlet. Why not
try painting or
learning how to
play an instrument?
There are a variety
of websites,
magazines and
organisations that
can help you get
started.

ANSATXT: As well as attending social events, you could try signing up with an introductions agency or placing an ad in a newspaper or magazine. Most of all, keep an open mind and a positive attitude — being happy makes you attractive.

ANSATXT: Try
talking to your
friends and
family. Often
when people feel
isolated, it is
because they
choose to be so.
Professional
counselling is
also an option,
even if you just
need someone to
talk to.

ANSATXT:
Definition: (n.)
the state or
quality of being
alive.

Acknowledgements

The writers would like to thank Simon Prosser, Francesca Main, Ross Sutherland, Chris Hicks, Tim Clare, Joe Dunthorne, John & Annette Wright, Scott Wright, Steve & Janet Stickley, all the Norwich writers, Elizabeth Sheinkman, all at the Port Eliot Lit Fest, Sally Roe, Fran Stapleton and Jeanette Tyndall.

He just wanted a decent book to read ...

Not too much to ask, is it? It was in 1935 when Allen Lane, Managing Director of Bodley Head Publishers, stood on a platform at Exeter railway station looking for something good to read on his journey back to London. His choice was limited to popular magazines and poor-quality paperbacks – the same choice faced every day by the vast majority of readers, few of whom could afford hardbacks. Lane's disappointment and subsequent anger at the range of books generally available led him to found a company – and change the world.

'We believed in the existence in this country of a vast reading public for intelligent books at a low price, and staked everything on it'
Sir Allen Lane, 1902–1970, founder of Penguin Books

The quality paperback had arrived – and not just in bookshops. Lane was adamant that his Penguins should appear in chain stores and tobacconists, and should cost no more than a packet of cigarettes.

Reading habits (and cigarette prices) have changed since 1935, but Penguin still believes in publishing the best books for everybody to enjoy. We still believe that good design costs no more than bad design, and we still believe that quality books published passionately and responsibly make the world a better place.

So wherever you see the little bird – whether it's on a piece of prize-winning literary fiction or a celebrity autobiography, political tour de force or historical masterpiece, a serial-killer thriller, reference book, world classic or a piece of pure escapism – you can bet that it represents the very best that the genre has to offer.

Whatever you like to read – trust Penguin.